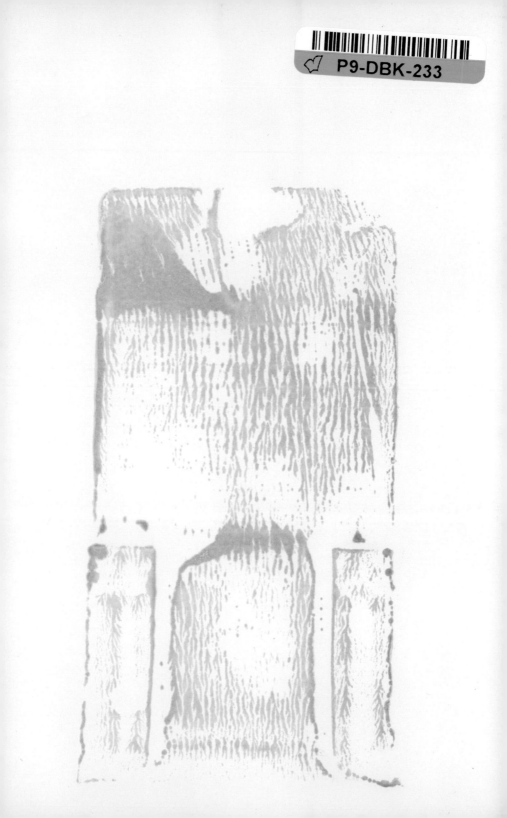

LATIN POETRY
BEFORE AND AFTER

LATIN POETRY

Before and After

by

CLARENCE W. MENDELL

ARCHON BOOKS
1970

SBN: 208 00844 6

Library of Congress Catalog Card Number: 70–96730

Printed in the United States of America

Contents

Preface

The present volume is the third in a series of three the purpose of which is to present to the general reader who, without a specific or technical acquaintance with the Latin poets, has nevertheless an intelligent background sufficient for an appreciation of them and some curiosity to know better what they wrote and how the poetry which they produced began, developed, and changed in the course of time—a better understanding of that process. In addition the series aims to give the reader a better understanding of what these poets have contributed to the literature of our own time and how this contribution was transmitted to the medieval world when the Roman Empire, its native setting, ceased to exist. The first volume dealt with the last century before Christ, the second with the first century after. The present volume is called "Before and After" because it attempts to show how the poets of the first were possible at all and how those of the second were made adaptable to a different world. As in the first two volumes, so in the present one, the translations are by the author and only such Latin is quoted as is necessary to clarify specific points.

LATIN POETRY

BEFORE

CHAPTER ONE

The Primitive Latin Verse

IT IS TRADITIONAL to say that Roman poetic literature began with the translation of the Odyssey by a Greek slave captured at Tarentum and used as schoolmaster to the children of his Roman master, whence his hybrid name, Livius Andronicus. This is partially true, but only partially. There are many indications of native "poetic" creations before 264 when Livius Andronicus presumably came to Rome. For one thing, the meter into which Andronicus translated the Odyssey is not Greek but native Italian. For another, when Andronicus was accorded recognition and given a place on the Aventine for meetings of the "poets' guild" who were the other members of the guild?

Let us first consider the matter of meter. It was called Saturnian verse, indicating that it was considered primitive or at least prehistoric, native to the soil. That it was accentual and not quantitive is indicated by the crude dances or rather marchings with which it was associated.

The oldest fragment that we have is the song of the Arval Brothers, an ancient college of priests, one of whose functions it was to bless the first fruits at their festival in May. The tablet on which it was found is of course much later in date than the ritual which it records amongst the acts of the brotherhood but such ritual songs were preserved most conservatively at Rome. From our point of view, the understanding of the Saturnian verse, it is unsatisfactory because it is not in regular stanzas. This is the "song" as we have it:

Enos, Lares, iuvate (thrice repeated)
Neve lue rue sins incurrere in pleores (thrice)
Satur fu, fere Mars, Limen sali (thrice)
Sta, berber (thrice)
Semunis alterne advocapit conctos (thrice)
Enos, Marmor, iuvato. (thrice)
Triumpe, triumpe, triumpe, triumpe, triumpe.

Help us, Lares, help us. (thrice)
And thou Mars let not plague and ruin come on the people
          (thrice)
Be sated, cruel Mars. Leap over the threshold (thrice)
Halt. Beat the ground. (thrice)
Call alternately on all the heroes. (thrice)
Help us, Mars. (thrice)
Bound, Bound, Bound, Bound, Bound.

There is little to be learned from this song about the Saturnian
verse except that it falls into no category of Greek meter and
that it can be most easily read by using the normal word accent,
disregarding the unaccented syllables.

A further step may be taken by considering the epitaphs of the
Scipios discovered in the eighteenth century in the family mauso-
leum. The earliest dates from 280 B.C.

Cornelius Lucius Scipio Barbatus
Gnaivod patre prognatus, fortis vir sapiensque
Quoius forma virtutei parissuma fuit
Consol censor aedilis quei fuit apud vos
Taurasia Cisauna Samnio cepit.
Subigit omne Loucanam opsidesque abdoucit.

Cornelius Lucius Scipio Barbatus
Whose father was Gnaeus, a brave man and wise
Whose handsome appearance was equal to his valor
Who was consul, censor, aedile amongst you.
He captured Taurasia, Cisauna, Samnium,
He subdued all Lucana and led off hostages.

Here we have at least a definite purpose to construct regular lines, approximately similar each to each. The problem is: what is the line and wherein lies the similarity? Accepting our conclusion that the basis of the Saturnian verse is accentual and that the accents fall where they fall in the normal prose pronunciation of the words, we find that the first line of the epitaph reads: *Cornélius Lúcius Scípio Barbátus,* with four accents. But the second line, *Gnaívod pátre prognátus, fórtis vír sapiénsque,* has six accents. The third has five: *Quoíus fórma virtútei paríssuma fúit.* The fourth has six, the fifth four, and the last line six. This irregularity is general throughout the epitaphs and also in the few lines quoted by grammarians from the translation of the Odyssey into Saturnians by Livius Andronicus. It should be noted in passing that all the lines seem metrically to fall into two parts which may or may not have the same number of accents. One more dependable basis for consideration is given by the fact that the grammarians regularly cite one particular line as the model of the Saturnian verse: *Dábunt málum Metélli Naévio poétae.* They therefore looked upon this arrangement of three accents in the first half of the line and two in the second as the correct one. It seems reasonable therefore to conclude that the fundamental line of Saturnian verse was based on accent, not on quantity, and consisted of two parts, of which the first had three accents, the second two, and that the number (as well as the quantity) of the intervening syllables was ignored. This is a primitive type of verse but not inconsistent with its very early, primitive origin.

Something more must be said about Livius Andronicus himself for he was undoubtedly considered to have been the *fons et origo* of Latin literature. How old he was when he was brought to Rome we have no way of telling beyond the fact that he was old enough to be the tutor of young children. The capture of Tarentum occurred in 275 B.C. In addition to his translation of the Odyssey, he translated at least ten Greek tragedies and wrote the hymn to celebrate a Roman victory at Sena in 267. As a reward for this he was assigned a room on the Aventine to be the meeting place of the guild of poets. The Aventine was largely the abode of foreigners and the guild members had no social standing at Rome. That the games for which Livius wrote his hymn were the saecular games (recalling Horace's *Carmen Saeculare*) seems plausible from the fact that these games were also once called the *ludi Tarentini* and that Livius from Tarentum would be a logical choice to write the hymn. Poetry was not the occupation of free citizens until the era of the "New Poets."

Not much more is known of the life of Gnaeus Naevius, a younger contemporary of Livius. His dates are approximately 269–204 B.C. Tradition placed his birthplace in Campania where he may have had early contact with the Greek literature current in that district south from Naples. He fought in the first war against Carthage. He wrote tragedies and comedies about which we know nothing save that through them he got into trouble with the family of the Metelli, whence the line discussed above: *dabunt malum Metelli Naevio poetae.* He seems to have been jailed and later released but spent his last years in self-imposed exile at Utica where he wrote an epic on the subject of the First Punic War in Saturnian verse, of which only fragments survive. It would be in keeping with the arrogance implicit in his other doings to have written his own epitaph as quoted by grammarians:

> Immortales mortales si foret fas flere
> Flerent divae Camenae Naevium poetam:
> Itaque postquam est in Orco traditum thensauro
> Obliti sunt Romae loquier lingua Latina.
>
> (from Aulus Gellius, 1.24.2.)

(Were it right for the immortals to weep for mortals the divine Muses would weep for the poet Naevius. For after he was consigned to the treasure house of Orcus they forgot at Rome how to speak in the Latin tongue.) In passing we should not overlook the persistent alliteration which will prove to be a popular characteristic of early Latin poetry.

CHAPTER TWO

Plautus

THE EARLIEST WRITER of Latin poetry of whose works we possess any considerable body is Titus Maccius Plautus, writer of popular comedies which provided him with a living. These plays were borrowings from or imitations of the Greek New Comedy, not of the Old Comedy of Eupolis, Cratinus, and Aristophanes. The New Comedy developed after the humiliation of Athens, when it was no longer safe to make sport of public characters and institutions. It was a comedy of lower class folk, a sort of comedy of manners, modelled to a considerable extent on the later and lesser plays of Euripides.

The chief exponent of the New Comedy was Menander and from him emanated Shakespeare's well-known phrase in which Hamlet, instructing the players, says: "for anything so overdone is from the purpose of playing whose end both at the first and now is to hold as 'twere the mirror up to nature." Shakespeare, by what route none can say, derived his phrase from the Roman commentator Donatus: *"imitatio vitae, speculum consuetudinis, imago veritatis."* Donatus ascribes it to Cicero but later restricts its application to comedy (the New Comedy) and credits the definition to Livius Andronicus. There is early confusion between the mirror and the image, between the reflector and the imitator, and Aristophanes of Byzantium exclaims: "Oh, Menander and Life, which of you was the imitator?" For our present purpose the point of interest is that the New Comedy aimed at reproducing the life of its time.

Plautus was born at Sarsina in Umbria about 250 B.C. Early in life he moved to Rome and worked as a stagehand until he had saved enough capital to engage in trade. Here he was unsuccessful, lost everything and hired out as a mill-hand to a baker. It was then that he discovered his facility in play writing at which he earned a living for the rest of his life. He died in Rome about 184 B.C.

Varro, the antiquarian scholar of the first century before Christ, listed twenty-one plays out of more than a hundred ascribed to Plautus as surely genuine and of these we have twenty intact and fragments of the twenty-first. Roughly the plays fall into two major categories: those which portray some given type such as the *Aulularia* which depicts the miser and was the model for Moliere's *L'Avare*; and those which depend for amusement on general confusion (usually provoked by slaves) of which the best known is probably the *Menaechmi* in which the confusion is caused by the apparent identity of twin brothers and which inspired Shakespeare's *Comedy of Errors* and more recently *The Boys From Syracuse*. The second type was and always has been the more popular.

　▸ The plays were put on at the various national "games"—either regular events coming at specified times during the year, such as the Ludi Romani, the Ludi Plebei, the Ludi Megalenses, or special games celebrated as the result of a vow in honor of some god or games to do honor to a triumph or to some great man's funeral. These games were conducted by the aediles who bought from the playwrights the plays to be presented. They were given in the open. There was no theater in Rome until Pompey's theater, built in 55 B.C. Benches were put up temporarily for the audience and a stage which consisted merely of a wooden platform with a high wooden background made of plain unpainted wooden boards (the *scaena*) with doors for the necessary entrances and exits.

What seems rather strange to us as we read the plays of Plautus and Terence is that a great part of them was sung, either by the actors themselves or by special singers off-stage. The former suggests our modern musical comedies, but how the latter was accomplished is hard to visualise in view of the fact that the theater had no wings or orchestra pit. The facts however seem to be beyond question, since our manuscripts distinguish clearly spoken parts (*diverbia*) and singing parts (*cantica*).

The *Amphytrio* is the first of Plautus' plays (taking them alphabetically) and deals with the birth of Hercules. Jupiter has adopted as a disguise the form of Amphytrion who is away at war, while Mercury assumes the shape of Sosia, the slave of the absent master. Alcmena, Amphytrion's wife, is thoroughly deceived. A long prologue spoken by Mercury opens the play with tedious repetition designed to make everything clear to the restless audience. To spare the reader, I quote only parts of the prologue. (11. 13–32)

> So, if you'd have me ever approve and help withal
> Your profit making year by year, then keep
> Deep silence while this merry play goes on. For so
> You'll all be fair and equal judges of its worth.
> Now by whose orders and for what I come here now
> I'll tell you and my proper name I will disclose.
> I come at Jupiter's command; my real name's Mercury.
> My father sent me on an errand: I'm to-day
> To beg of you, although he well might order you—
> He knew you would obey his word for well he knew
> How much you fear him even as it well behooves you to—
> But still he bade me beg of you in kindly words
> For he at whose command I come, said Jupiter,
> Fears ill as much as each of you, born as he was
> Of father divine and earth born mother too: so 'tis
> Not to be wondered at if he at heart feels dread.
> And I as well, the son of this same Jupiter,
> Fear ill that from my mother comes to me. Wherefore
> I come in peace and that same peace I bring to you.
>
> This town you see is Thebes and in this dwelling here
> Amphytrio lives, of Argive father, born at Argos,
> And with him lives his wife Alcmena, daughter of
> Electrus. This Amphytrio now commands his legions,
> For the Theban folk are now at war with the Teleboians.
> Before he left here and betook him to the army
> He had made his wife Alcmena pregnant. I believe
> You know the sort of man my father always is

And how much freedom he allows himself in all
Such matters and what a lover he is when fancy takes him.
He fell in love with Alcmena without her husband's knowledge
And made her pregnant. So—to make all things clear to you
About Alcmena—she is now pregnant by them both,
Her husband and great Jupiter and he, my father,
Is bedded with her now within this very house,
And for this purpose he has lengthened out the night
To give himself a longer time for his own pleasure
And likewise he has disguised himself as Amphytrio.

Now on this day Amphytrio will be coming back
With Sosia his slave whose likeness I have taken.

But there with a lantern Sosia comes, Amphytrio's slave.
I'll keep him when he gets here from this dwelling house.

There is also a short epilogue to the *Amphytrio* spoken by
Jupiter. It is not typical of the epilogues to Plautus' plays. These
are usually addressed to the spectators and call for their applause.
Most frequently they consist of a single line by the final speaker
the gist of which is "the play is over, give your applause." In the
Amphytrio Jupiter returns to assure the home-coming captain
that all is well.

Be you at ease: I come, Amphytrio, to be
Of help to you and yours. No need for you to fear.
Have done with soothsayers, prophets, all of them, for I
Will tell you everything, what's past and what's to be,
Better than they for I am Jupiter. First, then,
I lay with your Alcmena and I made her pregnant
With a son. You too before you left to fight the war
Begat a son by her. She bare them both at one
Deliverance. The one that is the product of my seed
Shall by his deeds to you bring never dying glory.
Return you to your tranquil life with your Alcmena.
No blame does she deserve from you: 'twas by my force
She was compelled to this. I now return to heaven.

The *Asinaria* is a very different play from the *Amphytrio*. It is wholly earthy and farcical. An old man, Demaenetus, is bullied by his wife Artemona who holds the purse strings. Their son Argynippus is in love with a courtesan named Philaenium. The son appeals to his father and together they manage to divert the money which Artemona had destined for the purchase of a herd of asses. They buy the girl but a rival of the son, one Diabolus, reveals the business to the wife who breaks in on a supper of father, son, and mistress and drags the old man home. The prologue is short and merely sets forth the Greek origin of the play, promises a good show and appeals to the audience for support. The epilogue is shorter still and simply states that everyone would probably do as the old man did and that if the audience applauds he'll probably escape a beating.

The *Bacchides* is more complicated. Two young men at Athens fall in love with two courtesans who are sisters but curiously enough have the same name. The complications are caused by the wiles of a slave of one of the young men aimed first at getting the boy's father away from Athens and then, after further troubles caused by the second young man's confusion between the two Bacchides, at getting out of the old man the money to pay for the girls. When the two fathers learn the whole business the two girls wheedle them into a reconciliation and the play ends with all of them celebrating merrily together. There is no prologue and a very brief, rather moralising epilogue.

The *Captivi* is a complete contrast with the *Bacchides*. Plautus would seem to have been criticised for the loose morals of his plays and boasts that here is a play which is wholly moral and has not any of his hackneyed situations. He is right: it is perfectly moral and also pretty dull. His boast is made in a commendably short epilogue which is more than offset by an unconscionably long prologue. This is the plot. Hegio of Aetolia has two sons. One disappeared as a child. The other is captured by the Elians in a war with Aetolia. In the hope of getting the captive back by exchange Hegio buys up Elian prisoners, among them one Philocrates and his slave, Tyndarus. The slave is to be sent to effect the exchange in Elis. But master and slave have agreed to disguise themselves, each as the other, and thus Philocrates gets off safely. Hegio discovers the ruse and sends Tyndarus to the quarries. When the captive is brought back he brings with him a renegade slave who confesses that he had in the beginning stolen the youngster and that Tyndarus is he. Result, a happy family reunion.

The *Casina* derives its name from the heroine, a pretty slave girl who is being wooed by two fellow slaves in the household of the elderly Lysidamus. He supports one of the two hoping to get Casina for himself. The marriage is performed but, in place of the bride, the other slave who wanted her, Chalinus, disguised as a girl, impersonates the bride. Cleustrata, the wife of the old man, has been privy to the plot and mocks her husband gleefully. To shorten the play, as the playwright says, we are curtly informed that Casina is free-born, the long lost daughter of a neighbor and will be married to Lysidamus' son, Euthynicus. It is an astonishingly short and rather feeble play. Strangely enough, it seems to have been revived fifty years later and the prologue is that of the revival. This prologue is excessively long and, among other things, claims that the play on its first appearance was a huge success. This is hard to believe. The short epilogue foretells the happy future of the wedded pair.

The *Cistellaria*, or Treasure Box, is so named from the box of trinkets which has an important part in the play. This is one of Plautus' earliest productions, rather commonplace and noteworthy only for the fact that it contains a considerable amount of singing. Demipho had, eighteen years before the action opens, violated a free-born girl in Sicyon. Returning to his native Lemnos, he had married and been left a widower with one daughter. He returned to Sicyon and married the girl whom he had wronged and who had meanwhile borne a daughter and exposed her. This daughter, recovered by a courtesan, Melaenis, had been brought up as this woman's daughter, was called Selanium, and had become the mistress of a young man named Alcesimarchus. He was forced by his father to become engaged to Demipho's daughter. A well-disposed slave reveals Selanium's origin and she is reclaimed by her mother and married by her to Alcesimarchus. There is no prologue to the play but it has a rather unusual epilogue spoken by the cast of players.

Wait not, spectators, for us actors to come back.
No one will come again. We'll end our work within.
When that is done we'll doff our costumes. Afterwards
Those who have acted ill will get a beating. Those
Who have not done ill will get a drink. Now what is left
For you, spectators, that is left: follow the custom
Of all our ancestors: applaud the finished play.

The *Epidicus* (no prologue and a two-line epilogue) is named after the slave whose wily tricks cause the intricate complexities of the plot. It is unnecessary to follow these complexities throughout their course. They are of the usual sort, ill assorted love affairs, the cheating of stupid old men, discovery of long lost daughters, and so on. In the *Epidicus* they are all used *ad nauseam*.

It is a relief to turn to the *Menaechmi*, one of the best of the plays of Plautus, the model for Shakespeare's "Comedy of Errors." It is superior to the play of Shakespeare who sought to gild the lily by adding to the identical twins a pair of identical twin slaves. In Plautus' play the twins are separated when seven years old, one of them being stolen when on a trip with his father. The father died of grief. The grandfather who was very fond of the boys changed the name of the boy who returned home safe to that of the lost boy—Menaechmus. When he was grown up, this second Menaechmus, whose name had been Sosicles, goes searching everywhere for his lost brother, finally turning up in Epidamnus to which town his brother had actually been carried and where he had become a respected citizen. In Epidamnus the twins are constantly confused by everyone, furnishing the comic situations of the play. The *Menaechmi* has a long prologue which gives a good summary of the plot. The only epilogue is the last line of the last speaker. (Since the Menaechmi is translated entire in the Appendix, I give no extracts here.)

The *Mostellaria*, the Haunted House, without prologue and with only the last line of the final speaker as epilogue, presents an old man of Athens, Theopropides, who has been away from home for some time. In his absence, his son Philolaches has been hitting the high spots with his friends. In the middle of a drinking bout they are startled to hear that Theopropides has returned. Philolaches' slave Tranio, the real hero of the play, takes charge of the situation.

> PH. Here comes the feast—look there. Here's Tranio coming to us from the harbor.
> TR. Philolaches. PH. What now TR. Both I and you—
> PH. What of I and you? TR. We're lost.
> PH. What's that? TR. Your father's come. PH. Where? I beg of you. TR. We're ruined quite.
> PH. Who said so then, who saw him? TR. I did: so I'm telling you. PH. Alas,
> What am I doing? TR. Why the hell ask what you're doing? You're lying down.
> PH. You saw him? TR. I myself, I tell you. PH. Are you sure? TR. Yes, sure. PH. I'm done for
> If you are telling the truth. TR. What good could it do me to tell you a lie?
> PH. What am I going to do? TR. Have all this truck cleared out away from here.
> Who's that asleep there? PH. Callidamates. TR. Delphinium, wake him up.
> DEL. Callidamates, I say, wake up. CAL. I'm awake—give me a drink.
> DEL. Wake up. Philolaches' father's back from overseas. CAL. Then farewell, father.
> PH. He's faring well enough but I'm undone. CAL. How can you be undone?
> PH. By Pollux, I beg you, get up. Father's coming. CAL. You say your father's coming?
> Tell him to go away again. Why should he want to come back home?

Tranio herds the revellers into the house, secures the door, and, meeting Theopropides, tells him that the ghost of a murdered man is within and is preventing everyone from entering. At this point the money lender who has financed Philolaches turns up and demands his money back.

TH. Oh Neptune I am doubly grateful to you from my
 deepest heart
That you have let me get away from you in safety and alive.
But if hereafter in the future you should learn that I have gone
One foot's length out to sea then there's no reason why you
 should not do
To me what you have tried to do. So now farewell, begone
 from me,
For from this day I've trusted to you all that I shall ever
 trust.
TR. By Pollux, Neptune, you're at fault—you've missed your
 opportunity.
TH. After three long years I am coming back from Egypt to
 my home
And I believe that I shall come most welcome to my dear
 ones all.
TR. More welcome still would be the man reporting to us you
 were dead.
TH. What's this? The door is shut in daytime. I'll knock.
 Open up someone.
TR. Who's this now coming to our house? TH. Well, there at
 last is Tranio.
TR. Oh, Theopropides, my master, welcome. I'm glad you're
 safely back.
You're still well? TH. As you see. TR. That's fine. TH. But
 have the lot of you gone mad?
TR. How's that? TH. Why, here you walk about and no one
 answers when I knock.
I've almost broken down the door with beating. TR. Good
 god, you touched the door?
TH. Touched it? I beat upon it. TR. Oh dear. TH. What's
 the matter? TR. That is bad.
I can't begin to tell you what a terrible thing it is you've done.
TH. What now? TR. I beg you, run. Come right away from
 there. You touched the door?
TH. How could I knock, pray, without touching it? TR. By
 Hercules you've ruined

TH. Whom? TR. All your family. TH. May all the gods above avert that omen.

Tranio wards off the money lender with another lie but presently Theopropides learns the whole truth. Everything looks black but one of Philolaches' friends artfully persuades the old man to forgive all and join in the general celebration.

The *Persa* is a weak play of intrigue. Toxilus, a rascally slave, has, during the absence of his master from his home in Athens, bought a girl from a pander. To avoid paying for her he devises a plot with a poor, parasitical Athenian, Saturio. This man ostensibly offers his daughter for sale to the pander as a prisoner of war from Persia. A fellow slave of Toxilus poses in Persian costume as the girl's owner. The pander pays the price demanded. Then Saturio in great indignation marches in and demands justice from the magistrate. The pander is forced to give back the money and Toxilus with his friends celebrate with a merry feast.

The *Poenulus*, or Man From Carthage, is not only lacking in interest but the text has become confused in transmission. The scene is Kalydon and all the chief characters are of Carthaginian extraction. The play has a slight antiquarian interest from the fact that there are some phrases used which purport to be in the Punic language. There is a long prologue and no epilogue.

The *Pseudolus*, the Liar, is far better. Phoenicium is a courtesan owned by the pander, Ballio, and beloved by Callidorus. Ballio is ready to do business but a Macedonian soldier has already paid three quarters of the purchase price of the girl and is expected to pay the rest on the day on which the play opens. Pseudolus, a faithful slave of Callidorus, cheats the soldier who has been sent by the Macedonian to make the final payment, gets his letter of authorization, and, by disguising another slave as this soldier, procures Phoenicium for his master. The real soldier turns up and gets back from the pander the whole price of the girl. The pander has also, trusting in his own cleverness, made a bet that he will not be cheated. There is general rejoicing at the discomfiture of the pander. The play has a short prologue and no epilogue.

The *Rudens*, the Rope, is unique in two ways. The name has

no significance and the setting is by the seaside. An old man of Athenian origin named Daemones lives near Cyrene. Years before he has lost his only child, a daughter. On a morning after a storm, a young man named Plesidippus comes to Daemones' cottage inquiring for a pander named Labrax who has agreed to meet him at a temple of Venus, near the cottage of Daemones, to sell him a girl named Palaestra with whom he is in love. But Labrax does not turn up. Instead he sails for Sicily where, so he has heard, he can get a better price. His ship has however been wrecked in the storm. Palaestra and her maid Ampelisca are washed ashore and take refuge in the temple of Venus. Labrax gets ashore further along the beach. He tries to reclaim Palaestra but old Daemones, learning that her origin like his is Athenian, protects her. Meanwhile one of his slaves Gripus has gone out fishing and found a wallet containing Labrax's money and some of Palaestra's childhood ornaments. The fisherman agrees to give them back to Labrax, but Trachalio, Plesidippus' slave, intervenes and the matter is referred to Daemones for judgment. He recognizes the childish trinkets as his long lost daughter's. Labrax is forced to give up Palaestra but gets his money back through a deal by which he frees Ampelisca. Gripus and Trachalio are set free by their respective masters, Trachalio marries Ampelisca, and Palaestra and Plesidippus are married. All are joyously happy. The prologue is spoken by Arcturus, evidently to suggest the romantic tone of the play. There is no epilogue.

The *Stichus* is a strange piece with practically no plot and unusually short. It tells of two wives in Athens whose husbands have long been away. They remain faithful although their father urges them to marry again. Finally their husbands return safe and prosperous and the rest of the little piece consists of the rejoicing of the two households, especially of the slave Stichus who provides the name for the "play." There is no prologue and no epilogue.

The *Trinummus*, or Three Penny Piece, returns to the comedy of intrigue. Charmides, an old man of Athens, has occasion to leave home for a considerable period and, not trusting his son Lesbonicus, gives to an old friend Callicles the secret of a considerable treasure which he has hidden away. Lesbonicus, a genial rake, runs through what money he has and sells the house to get more. Callicles buys the house to save the treasure. A very eligible young man named Lysiteles wishes to marry Lesbonicus' sister. To obtain a dowry for her Lesbonicus prepares to make over to her a small family estate near Athens. Callicles realizes that this will leave the boy penniless and hires for three drachmae (hence the name of the play) a parasite to pretend to be a messenger from Charmides and to give Lesbonicus a goodly amount of money taken from the treasure. The return of Charmides winds up all difficulties and, to complete his happiness, Lesbonicus is provided with a suitable wife of his father's choosing. There is a moderate prologue spoken by Luxury and Poverty, again apparently with the purpose of setting the tone. There is no epilogue.

The *Vidularia* (The Wallet) is in such fragmentary state as to be of little or no value. It appears only in a palimpsest manuscript spoiled by chemicals and does not merit discussion.

From the plays of complicated trickery and badinage we now turn to the five plays whose purpose would seem rather to present some particular type of character. The first of these (again following the alphabetical order) is the *Aulularia* (The Treasure). The text of the play is incomplete but there is an epilogue which would indicate that, at the time at which the manuscript was written, the text as it is was thought to be complete.

> Wait not, spectators, for our actors to come back.
> No one will come again: they'll end their work within.
> When that is done they'll doff their costumes. Afterwards
> Those who have acted badly will be thrashed and those
> Who've not done ill will get a drink. Now what is left
> For you, spectators, that is left: follow the custom
> Of all our ancestors: applaud the finished play.

(The identical epilogues to the *Cistellaria* and the *Aulularia* indicate that Plautus used a stock form for these epilogues, considering them no part of the play itself.) The plot is laid in Lemnos. Euclio, the miser, has found a treasure but continues to live as if in extreme poverty. A rich neighbor, seeing this, proposes to marry Euclio's daughter without a dowry. The preparations for the wedding feast give Euclio much concern and in fact the pot of gold is stolen. Also the daughter, who has been violated by his own nephew, bears a child. The thief turns out to be the slave of the nephew who, with the consent of all, marries the girl and restores the treasure. The plot is weak indeed but the character of the miser is fairly well drawn.

The *Curculio* (literally, The Weevil) is the nickname of a parasite, the central figure of the play. The scene is laid in Epidauris. A young man, Phaedromus, is in love with a courtesan, Planasium, owned by a shrewd pander. To raise the money to buy the girl Phaedromus sends the parasite Curculio to borrow it from a friend in Caria. Curculio fails in this mission but manages to get the signet ring of a soldier who is also in love with Planasium and has deposited the money for her purchase with a banker in Epidaurus. Curculio forges a letter to the banker and Planasium is bought but with a guarantee that the money shall be returned if Planasium turns out to be free-born. When all seems to be going well the soldier returns and sues the banker and the pander. Suddenly the soldier discovers, by means of a ring of his own and one that Planasium wears, that she is his own sister, kidnapped years before. He recovers the money and agrees to the marriage of Planesium and Phaedromus. The parasite assumes credit for everything. This is by no means one of Plautus' better plays.

Scarcely better is the *Mercator*, the picture of a young business man of Athens, Charinus. Sent abroad by his father on a business trip, he falls in love with a courtesan, Pasicompsa, whom he buys and brings home, pretending that she is a present to his mother to be a servant maid. But his father, Demipho, immediately falls in love with Pasicompsa and, saying that she is too pretty to be a servant, proposes to get rid of her. Charinus is afraid to object openly and Demipho gets the girl away to the house of his friend Lysimachus. Lysimachus' wife however becomes jealous and the whole business is exposed. Charinus, instead of going off again on business as he had planned, stays at home and woos and wins Pasicompsa.

Much better as a play is the *Miles Gloriosus*, the Braggart Soldier. The hero, Purgopolynices, comes back from the wars to his home in Ephesus with a quantity of money and determined to enjoy himself. His mistress, Philocomasium, is in love with a

young civilian, Pleusicles, who is equally in love with her. They
meet in the house next door where she pretends to be her own
twin sister. They persuade Purgopolynices that a lady of good
standing is in love with him. Thereupon he pays Philocomasium
a large sum of money to comfort her and then he sends her away.
She and Pleusicles sail happily off to Athens. Meanwhile Purgopolynices pursues his suit of the supposed "lady" who is of course
a courtesan hired by the departed lovers. A jolly old man named
Periplectomenus who is in on the game pretends to be the "lady's"
husband and gives Purgopolynices a frightful scare.

The *Truculentus* (The Boor) is one of the last of the plays of
Plautus and lacks his merry outlook on life. There is not a like-
able character throughout. A courtesan Phronesium in Athens
has been generously supported by Diniarchus whom she discards
when his money is gone. She next becomes the mistress of a
soldier who has been away at war. To hold him she pretends to
bear him a child, using an abandoned infant for the purpose.
Meanwhile she pursues a young country fool whose slave is the
Boor of the title. This slave is captivated by Phronesium's maid
and gives up his protests against his master's behavior. The abandoned infant turns out to be the child of Diniarchus and a free-
born woman whom he had raped. He now marries her and
acknowledges the child but still cherishes the hope of reconciliation
with Phronesium.

Such a survey of the plays of Plautus cannot fail to produce a
feeling of boredom at the overall sameness of the plots in spite
of a variation of detail. We cannot but wonder at the lack of
imagination to create something new to enthrall an audience sated
with slave intrigue, stupid old men, and unscrupulous courtesans.
But this is to overlook at least two important facts. In early Rome
—actually in the Rome of all periods—theaters did not cater to
the public with daily performances. Plays were produced only at
the "games", perhaps a dozen times a year, so that the sense of
monotony was reduced and even perhaps a certain anticipation
aroused at the thought of seeing once more the old familiar show.
A perhaps not too remote analogy is the modern circus and this
analogy brings us to the second important fact suggested above.
The comedy of Plautus was not written for the Roman intellectuals.

They made no part of the holiday crowd at the Roman "games."
The mob that watched—often restlessly—the plays of Plautus
was almost completely composed of the illiterate, the unprivileged.
In other words, it was the uncritical proletariat.

It is clear, I think, why comedy never developed into anything
that was popular with Roman intellectuals. Shakespeare, who knew
both the pit and the gallery, could find the essential humor in
Plautus and make it over into something acceptable to both.

The plays of Plautus were presented off and on at Rome down
to the days of Diocletian, that is through the third century A.D.,
but no other great writer of comedy emerged. It is true that the
Scipionic Circle had tried to make something of the plays of their
protégé, Terence, but he proved to be caviar to the general and
the Circle was not really interested in his product.

Plautus still stands today as the one true exponent of Latin
Comedy and is still good reading if taken in small doses.

CHAPTER THREE

Terence

PLAUTUS HAD APPEALED to the rabble which flocked to the public games where his plays were produced. His boisterous humor and bawdy scenes were quite to their taste. Not so the comedies of the other great Latin comedian whose works we possess. Publius Terentius Afer, or Terence as he is better known to us was, as we have already noted, caviar to the general. His prologues were addressed to the literary group at Rome and discussed the literary character of his plays. His style was more austere, his humor less earthy than those of his popular and uninhibited predecessor.

Terence was born in Africa as his surname indicates. (*Afer* means a native of Africa, not a Carthaginian.) He was a slave, the property of a Roman senator, Terentius Lucanus, who was captivated by the boy's native beauty and, setting him free, gave him a good education. The next that is heard of Terence he has become a protégé of the Scipionic Circle and has written plays which, because of the purity of their Latin, were suspected of having been edited (or even written) by Scipio and Laelius. Before he was twenty-five he had written the six plays which have come down to us intact. At that point in his life he left Rome for a trip to Greece and died either there or on the trip home, in 159 B.C.

The *Andria* (The Girl from Andros, more familiarly known since the appearance of Thornton Wilder's play as The Woman of Andros) was the first of the six plays, appearing in 166 B.C., and is set in Athens as are all Terence's plays. An old man named Sino has a son Pamphilus who has acquired as mistress a young girl, Glycerium, originally from Andros, who had been friendless and alone until adopted by a courtesan from Andros, now dead. Sino and his old friend Chremes had planned a marriage between Pamphilus and Chremes' daughter. Chremes, however, hearing about Pamphilus' liaison with Glycerium, calls off the engagement. Hoping to reform his son, he tells him that the wedding plans are being completed. Davus, Pamphilus' slave, informs his master of the situation and Sino therefore unexpectedly receives the dutiful agreement of his son. He is startled but not at the end of his resources. He induces Chremes to change his mind and the wedding preparations become real and soon are near completion. But Davus too is resourceful. Glycerium has given birth to a child and this baby Davus places on Sino's doorstep where Chremes cannot fail to see it. This is too much for him and again he forbids the wedding. Everything is in a mess when one Crito appears from nowhere as a sort of god from the machine and proves that Glycerium is in reality Chremes' own long lost daughter. The wedding bells ring out and the general joy is made complete by the marriage of the other daughter of Chremes to a friend of Pamphilus who has long been in love with her.

The *Hecyra*, Mother-in-law, was put on in 165 and was far from being popular. It lacks action to an extreme degree. A young man at Athens named Pamphilus is forced by his father to abandon his mistress, Bacchis, and marry a nice young girl named Philomena. While Pamphilus is away on a trip out of town he discovers that he really loves Philomena who has returned to her father's house during her husband's absence. When Pamphilus comes back he finds that Philomena has born a son too soon after the marriage to be his own. His father meanwhile has gotten the idea that his wife Sostrata (the mother-in-law of the title) has driven Philomena out of his house and back to her own father out of dislike for the girl. The old lady does her best to reconcile her son and Philomena, but, while he keeps her secret, Pamphilus refuses to live with her again. Bacchis is the goddess from the machine. With the help of a lucky recognition by means of a ring she manages to clear up the situation. Pamphilus, it seems, had violated Philomena at a wild nocturnal festival some time before his marriage and is after all the father of the child. This solution appeases everyone and there is a general reconciliation.

The *Heauton Timoroumenos*, the Self Torturer, produced in 163, is again a play without much action. Chremes is an old man who has a son Clitipho whom he believes to be the embodiment of respectability but who is in fact the lover of an expensive courtesan named Bacchis. Meanwhile Chremes' neighbor, Menedemus, has driven his son Clinias from home by being too strict with him and, filled with remorse, has inflicted upon himself as penance a life of deprivation and hardship. Presently Clinias returns, unable to stand the separation from his own love, Antiphila, the daughter of old Chremes. Clitipho and Clinias between them, with the help of a rascally slave Syrus, concoct a scheme to satisfy the desires of both. Menedemus, in his contrite state, can refuse nothing to Clinias and is easily persuaded to do what he asks. He allows his son to bring into the house Bacchis whom he thinks to be his son's mistress and, along with her, her maids, one of whom is Antiphila in disguise. But it cannot long be concealed that Bacchis is Clitipho's mistress and not Clinias' and recriminations follow. In the midst of the disaster it is discovered than Antiphila is in reality Chremes' daughter who had been exposed years before as an unwanted girl baby. Clinias can be and is honorably engaged to Antiphila and, to keep him out of further trouble, a suitable wife is found for Clitipho. The slave Syrus is forgiven and all ends happily.

The *Eunuchus*, the Eunuch, 161 B.C., is surprisingly full of action for Terence. In spite of the name of the play and that of one of the characters, Thais, the scene of the *Eunuchus* is Athens. Thraso (not unlike the braggart soldier Purgopolynices of Plautus) is in love with a courtesan by the name of Thais who has a second lover, poorer but younger, Phaedria. This young man has a brother, Chaerea, who is madly in love with one Pamphila who is supposed to be Thais' sister but is really a slave given to Thais by Thraso. Chaerea puts on the clothes of a eunuch whom Phaedria is giving as a present to Thais and so gets into the women's quarters and there disports himself outrageously. Thais, in spite of a promise to Thraso to confine her attentions to him, gives her favors also to Phaedria. Parmeno, a confidential slave advising the two young men, stirs things up in the household of Thais. Everyone there denounces the false eunuch while Phaedria terrorizes the real one.

Thraso tries to take Pamphila back by force because Thais has played him false. But Thais has discovered that Pamphila is really the sister of a young Athenian citizen named Chremes (in spite of the traditional practice of using that name only for an *old* man). Thais and Chaerea drive off Thraso. Pamphila becomes engaged to Chaerea and Thais becomes a client of Phaedria's father and so accessible to the young man. All are happy except Thraso.

The *Phormio*, also produced in 161 B.C., is perhaps the best known of the plays of Terence, possibly because of its having no procurers or courtesans, and because, being in Terence's pure and simple Latin, it has been used in England (and sometimes in America too) as a school text along with or instead of Caesar. Antipho, a young Athenian, during his father's absence from town falls in love with a charming young girl, Phanium, poor and of unknown parentage but claiming to be a free-born Athenian. With the connivance of his slave Geta, Antipho concocts a scheme to get himself forced to marry Phanium. A parasite, Phormio is hired to claim the girl's acquaintance and to demand in court that Antipho, presented as her nearest of kin, be compelled to marry her. Antipho makes no defense and the court issues the order. Antipho's father returns to town and tries to get Phormio to withdraw his claim and take the girl away. Phormio pretends indignation at any such treatment of a respectable girl. Meanwhile Geta is called off to help elsewhere. A cousin of Antipho, Phaedria by name, wants him to raise some five thousand dollars to buy a flute girl with whom he is in love. Geta tells Antipho's father that Phormio will yield for five thousand dollars. The old man refuses to pay more than four thousand, but his brother Chremes, Phaedria's father, contributes the whole amount because he wants Antipho to marry his own daughter. This girl is the child of a woman of Lemnos whom Chremes had married unbeknownst to his Athenian wife, Nausistrata. It turns out that Antipho's girl is the daughter of Chremes and that her mother is dead. Antipho is rapturously happy and Phaedria too, for when Phormio tells Nausistrata about Chremes' double life she is glad enough to be informed to forget the five thousand dollars and forgive everyone except Chremes.

The last play of Terence, the *Adelphi*, the Brothers, was produced in 160 B.C. Two elderly brothers, Demea and Micio, are opposites in character, the former rigid in his integrity and frugal in his way of life, the latter easy going and inclined to enjoy the best. Demea has two sons of whom, in his frugality, he keeps one, Ctesipho, at home and gives the other, Aeschinus, to be adopted by Micio. Ctesipho is raised in rigorous discipline and hard work and his father considers him a paragon of virtue. He constantly complains that Micio is spoiling Aeschinus. There would seem to be some truth in the complaint for Aeschinus violently breaks into the house of a pander and kidnaps a harp girl. Micio refuses to intervene although he has some inward doubts. There is a scene with the indignant pander and it transpires that Aeschinus was all the time acting on Ctesipho's behalf and that it was Ctesipho's love for the harp girl that was behind the brawl. In the meantime Aeschinus has been having an affair with a free-born girl whom he has promised to marry. The girl's relations begin to make trouble for the girl is with child by Aeschinus. Micio for once becomes firm and insists that Aeschinus marry the girl. When Demea hears what his model son Ctesipho has been up to he is in a mighty rage. Micio succeeds in calming him down with a good dinner. Demea admits that he has been too strict and tries to show affability on all sides. He even persuades Micio, by using the man's own words, to marry Aeschinus' new mother-in-law. All ends happily.

Two characteristics which distinguish sharply the comedies of Terence from those of Plautus are, first and foremost, that the spirit is far less rollicking and gay. The plays of Plautus are uninhibited and appealed to the mob. Those of Terence are definitely more staid and were intended to please the literary circle which had made him their protégé. Second and scarcely less important, the Latin of Terence is of the purest, a surprising feature in the work of a man of foreign birth and speech but quite in keeping with his relations with the Scipionic Circle. It is this purity of Latin which has long made Terence a text book in English public schools.

Closely allied to this purity of style is the fact already mentioned that the prologues in Terence do not so much introduce the play and the characters to the audience as defend the author in some of his literary practices and attack his detractors—who must

have been numerous. Such for example is the prologue of the
Andria which defends the practice of "contaminatio", the merging
of two Greek plays to produce the Latin one.

> When first our poet had turned his mind to writing plays
> He thought the only object he must strive to gain
> Was that the plays he'd written should please the populace.
> But now he knows how differently the matter stands.
> For when he writes his prologue now its function is
> No more to tell the story but to meet the abuse
> Of some malevolent old poet in criticism.
> So listen now and hear the gist of their abuse.
> Menander wrote an Andria and he also wrote
> Perinthia. Whoever knew the one knew both
> For they are quite alike in argument but not
> In speech and style. Our poet admits he freely took
> In writing his own Andria lines as well from out
> Perinthia. This they criticize as bad and say
> One must not use "contamination" in one's plays.
> When so they say they're likewise bringing charge against
> Old Naevius, Plautus, Ennius as well whom this
> Our poet considers his models and would rather ape
> Their faults than these men's picayune busyness.
> So now to keep them quiet I warn them to desist
> From evil speaking or they'll learn their own mistakes.
> Give me your favor and apply your minds to knowing
> What hope you still may have of seeing new plays of his
> Invention or perchance must first demand of him.

The type of militant prologue which attacks the critics or, as
Terence insists, defends the author against attacks is well illustrated
by the *Phormio*.

> As long as the old poet cannot persuade our poet
> To withdraw from his pursuit and quietly retire
> He now is setting out to frighten him from writing
> With maledictions: keeps on saying the plays he writes
> Are tenuous in their matter, weak in point of style

Because he nowhere has presented a young man
Gone mad who sees a fleeing deer in terror chased
By hunting dogs and begging him with tears to help.
If he but knew that when his first play made a hit
'Twas by the actors' work it passed not its worth
He'd be less bold in attacking what he now attacks.
And if there's any listening here that says or thinks
That if the old poet had not first reviled our poet
Our own poet could not then have thought of anything
To make into a prologue, if he'd had no one
To curse against in turn, to that the answer's this:
The prize is open to all who follow the trade of poet.
The old poet tried to hound our poet until he starved;
Our poet has only answered, never launched attack.
If he had wanted to compete in compliments
He'd have had kindly answers. Now he'd better know
He's getting back again only what he has started.
Now I will make an end of talking about him
Though I am sure he'll make no end of doing ill.

Plautus and Terence were by no means the only writers of comedy at Rome. The rest, however, are little but names to us, cited by later annotators and commentators. The earliest we hear of was Caecilius who flourished about 179–168 B.C. Forty-two titles of his plays are cited and he is said to have followed his Greek models closely. Ennius was evidently unsuccessful in two attempts at comedy writing and Naevius also failed. There are not a few names known to us without any further knowledge of their work: Licinius, Atilius, Turpilius, Trabea, Lanuvinus, Juventius, Vatronius. About three others we know a little more: Titinius, Atta, and Afranius. All three presented plays in Roman dress, not in Greek. Atta was read by Horace. Of Afranius we have forty titles, three of which would seem to suggest some originality: The Divorce, Saved from the Sea, and The Pretender. None of this affords a real picture of what must have been an active trade in comedies for the games.

From the beginning tragedy was never popular with the Roman

populace. It received some attention from the litterati but not enough to preserve for us a single Latin tragedy written earlier than the first century A.D., and it is doubtful whether the plays of that era were not intended for reading rather than for acting. In the period now under consideration we have only a list of failures. Livius Andronicus is said to have translated a few tragedies. Naevius and Ennius made feeble attempts. Pacuvius, born at Brindisi, was a nephew of Ennius. At Rome he produced tragedies of which we have thirteen titles including an *Antigone*, an *Hermione*, a *Pentheus* and a *Teucer*. After living for a time in Rome he retired to Tarentum and died there about 130 B.C. Accius, slightly younger than Pacuvius, was held by all critics to be the greatest of Roman tragedians. He was a friend of Cicero and is mentioned three times by Horace. Especially noteworthy is Horace's phrase in his *Ars Poetica*: "The noble trimeters of Accius." Euripides was his favorite source. We have forty-seven titles, among them: *Alcestis, Andromeda, Antigone, Clytemnestra, Medea, Meleager* and *Telephus*. After Accius, we have the names only of four tragedians: Strabo, Pompilius, Titius, and Santius. Such is the meager history of early Roman Tragedy.

CHAPTER FOUR

Ennius

SOME TEN YEARS younger than Plautus and considerably older than Terence, the third of the four real giants of Rome's early days of literary significance, Quintus Ennius, was born at Rudini in Calabria in 239 B.C. He died at Rome in 169. Proud of the Roman citizenship (which he was later to attain) Ennius wrote of himself: "I who am Roman now was once Rudinian." With no pretence of humility, he wrote his own epitaph to appear on the tomb of the Scipios where he was buried.

> Behold the image of great Ennius
> Who wrote the story of your ancestors.
> Let no one weep nor honor me with tears:
> I flit still living on the lips of men.

He fought against Sardinia in 215 as a centurion of auxiliaries and in this action attracted the attention of Cato who took him with him to Rome. There he presently received his Roman citizenship. Earning his living by writing tragedies and comedies which, as we have seen, were largely unsuccessful, he seems to have lived in poverty or so it appeared to Cicero who commented on the poet in his essay on Old Age. Ennius' really impressive contribution to Latin literature was his eighteen-book epic on the history of Rome. It was composed in hexameter verse, the first ever written in Latin, and set the model for the meter of all subsequent epic. He called the work the *Annales* and it covered the period from the fall of Troy to his own day with the exception of one period, that of the First Punic War which Naevius had covered in Saturnian verse.

> Others have told the story in the measures
> Which fauns and poets used to tell their tales
> When none as yet had scaled the Muses' mount
> And none before me spake in studied phrase.

Inasmuch as we have lost at least ninety-five per cent of the epic and have to depend on fragments and on the statements of later writers, it is not possible to give a satisfactory account of the poem.

At or near the beginning came the description of a dream which the writer claims to have had in which the ghost of Homer appeared, convincing the poet that he was the reincarnation of Homer. Lucretius confirms this in his first book. The *Annales* told of the beginnings of Rome with Romulus presented as the grandson of Aeneas. The latest event to which we find reference occurred in 179 B.C.

Little enough tells us the sort of man Ennius was or how he lived. There is no reason to take seriously a jibe of Horace or a comment of Ennius himself, both of which present him as a heavy drinker. It was conventional at Rome to present poetry as produced by the inspiration of wine. Horace's contribution is: "Ennius himself the poet would never proceed to the telling / Of battles save in his cups." Ennius put it more succinctly: "I'm never a poet unless I have the gout." We do know that he tried his hand at many lesser products: an *Art of Dining* in hexameters, epigrams, an *Encomium of Africanus*, a poem of uncertain content called *Epicharmus* and another called *Euhemeros*. Finally he wrote what came to be called Satires but these are the special province of Lucilius and will be considered more at length in the next chapter.

What were the qualities of Ennius' great epic? Again we can judge only from the character of the remaining fragments and by the testimony of later writers. From the first we must conclude that, as was to be expected from a pioneer, these qualities were mixed, some bad, some good. We find, for example, lines consisting of six spondees, not with the purpose of producing any particular effect but in the ordinary course of the narrative. Typical examples are: *Cives Romani tunc facti sunt Campani* (The Campanians were then made Roman citizens); *Olli respondit rex Albai Longai* (To him responds the king of Alba Longa). There is also, according to the accepted canons of Latin usage, too much coincidence between word accent and verse accent: *Vires vitaque corpus meum nunc deserit omni* (All the strength and life now leaves my body). There is an unbearable amount of alliteration, as in *O Titi tute Tati tibi tanta, tyranne, tulisti* (How much you have endured, King Titus Tatius). On the other hand, there are lines of unquestionable power and imagination such as the much quoted *Postquam Discordia taetra / Belli ferratos postes portasque refregit* (When horrid Discord broke down the iron shod gates and portals of War). Here the personification of Discord and the figure of the doors of the Temple of Janus, closed in time of peace, show both imagination and the power to express it. It is perhaps not strange that we know more bad lines than good, since most of our fragments are from grammarians searching for faults. But occasional phrases do cause regret that we do not have more of the epic. *Stellis ardentibus aptum*, of the night sky studded with burning stars; *summo sonitu quatit ungula terram*, with mighty din the hoof shakes the earth; *semianimesque micant oculi lucemque requirunt*, Half alive the eyes flash and search for the light. These are but a few selected from an abundance.

Turning to the testimony of later writers, Lucilius, in the existing fragments, mentions Ennius at least four times, once as a second Homer. Cicero is the next witness. In his *Tusculan Disputations* he exclaims in his enthusiasm: "Oh splendid poet even though scorned by these singers of Euphorion" (who are of course the "new poets"). In *Pro Murena* he calls Ennius an excellent poet and a thoroughly dependable authority. Lucretius pays an unstinted tribute to Ennius in his first book: "So did our Ennius sing who first from the Mount of the Muses / Gathered from Helicon's hill the crown of leafage eternal, / Who through all the Italian folk should be famous forever." Horace is more discriminating and more convincing:

> From these lines which I write
> And those which once Lucilius wrote, if you remove
> The meters fixed and change the order, putting
> The first word last, the last word first, you'll not
> Find there the fragments of a dismembered poet
> As you will do if you dissolve the lines
> Of Ennius: *Postquam Discordia taetra*
> *Belli ferratos postes portasque refregit.*

Vergil never mentions Ennius but if imitation is the sincerest flattery his admiration must have been great. Conington finds more than fifty actual borrowings in the *Aeneid* and, while Conington is an enthusiastic source hunter, there can be no doubt that Vergil often went back to his great predecessor for both ideas and phrases. When the *Aeneid* superseded the *Annales* as the great national poem we hear no more of Ennius, but it should not be forgotten that Silius Italicus broke with the spirit of the Age of Rhetoric and returned to Ennius as his model.

The success of Ennius seems to have discouraged rivals but epic was not wholly neglected. One Matius translated the Iliad into hexameters. He was praised by Aulus Gellius and one fragment indicates his kinship with Ennius. Another epic writer mentioned by grammarians was Hostius who wrote a *Bellum Italicum*. Finally, Aulus Furius wrote *Annales* which seem to have been a supplement to those of Ennius.

CHAPTER FIVE

Lucilius

THERE HAS ALREADY been brief mention of Lucilius both toward the end of the first volume of this series and near the beginning of the second. This is altogether natural since Lucilius is in reality the connecting link between the two eras covered in those volumes. He was a member of the conservative Scipionic Circle which fathered Terence and he was the innovator who first expressed freely his own emotions and ideas in poetry and so inspired the self-expression of the "New Poets."

Gaius Lucilius was born of Latin status at Suessa Aurunca in 180 B.C. He never became a full Roman citizen, although his brother did, becoming a senator and the maternal grandfather of Pompey. Gaius Lucilius was comfortably off and became a friend of Scipio Africanus the younger and one of the later members of Scipionic Circle. He seems to have been active in the defense of the Italians after the agrarian legislation of Tiberius Gracchus. In gratitude for this support the town of Naples was to give him a public funeral as a benefactor. Lucilius served in the cavalry at Numantia (implying a certain amount of wealth). He died in 102 B.C. This is all that we know of the man who was the "inventor" of perhaps the most characteristic Roman literary product in verse, what later generations were to call the Satire. The name was probably first applied in derision to Horace's first book of Satires and then rather defiantly accepted by him; for its first occurrence as a literary term is in the first line of the second book, *Sunt quibus in Satura* ("There are those to whom in my Satire"). Before this Horace had referred to "the things which I write now and which once Lucilius wrote." How the word came to have an

offensive connotation is not hard to see. It is an adjective mean-
ing "stuffed with" and hence a rather motley mixture. We find it
applied somewhat frivolously to a platter of mixed first fruits, "lanx
satura", and again to a miscellaneous bill in the senate made up
of odds and ends of legislation of insufficient importance to war-
rant separate bills, an omnibus bill, "lex satura." After Horace
had given it the dignity of a literary title it was applied in retro-
spect to writings of Ennius and Lucilius.

It is Horace who gives us the best characterization of Lucilius'
work in two fairly long comments in his Satires. The first is from
the fourth Satire of Book I.

> Eupolis and Cratinus and Aristophanes also,
> All of the poets to whom we owe the Old Comedy's wisdom,
> If they beheld any man deserving of their indignation
> For being malicious, a thief, an adulterer, say, or a cutthroat
> Or what you will of that sort, denounced him with plenty
> of freedom.
> 'Tis from these poets that Lucilius wholly depends,
> these he follows
> Changing only the meters, both witty and keen on the tracking
> Down every scent, but harsh just the same in composing
> his verses.
> There he was surely at fault: in an hour while standing
> on one foot
> Often he wrote as a stunt two hundred or more of his verses.
> Since then he flowed along muddily, much that he wrote
> would you gladly
> Cut from the text. He was garrulous, lazy and loathe
> to encounter
> All the hard toil of writing, of writing well is my meaning.
> For of his writing a lot I care not—here's Crispinus
> would give me
> Odds of the best: "Take your tablets and I'll take mine; set a
> Time and a place, get your judges: we'll quickly determine the
> question
> Which of us two can write most in an hour." The gods
> were more kindly,
> Giving to me a mind that is slow and timid, producing

Little enough in words. But you, imitate if it please you
Wind shut up in the bellows till the fire has melted the iron.

Apparently Horace was subjected to some abuse for having
criticized Lucilius who was held by the literati to be the model
of this form. The literati in this case would seem to have been
"grammatici" or school teachers whom Horace held in little esteem
at best. He once said that he did not want to have his works
become a school book to be taught to girls by whining school
teachers. At any rate, on this occasion Horace did take umbrage
and, accepting the term which they had applied to his first book
(which ironically had borrowed much from Lucilius), he lashed
back at the grammatici in the first Satire of the second book.

I *did* say that Lucilius' verses ran unsmoothly,
Badly disordered in their scansion. Who, I ask you,
Can be so foolish in his admiration as to
Question this statement? In the selfsame Satire also
He was commended in that he also rubbed the city
Amply with salt. But, giving him this commendation,
Is not the same as granting him all other virtues.
For if it were I needs must praise as splendid poetry
Mimes of Liberius. So it is not enough to open
Mouths of the listeners in a laugh, though that, I grant you,
Is an achievement. There is also need of brevity
So that the sense runs on nor ever impedes its progress
By the intrusion of laborious words that weary
Ears of the tiring listener. There's the necessity also
Of varying style that now is serious, now is jesting,
Taking in turn the role of orator or poet, anon of
Urban irony, with purpose curbing its sharpness.
For the ridiculous is often even more potent
Than the more solemn to decide important questions.
This is a fact those ancient writers of "Old Comedy"
Knew to the full (and we should be their imitators),
Poets that the fop Hermogenes has never pondered
Nor yet that ape that sings but Calvus and Catullus.

Lucilius wrote thirty books of what later came to be known as Satires. The range of subject matter is as wide as the title suggests; an assembly of the gods to decide how to preserve the city of Rome, a journey from Rome to the Straits of Messina, questions of grammar, personal attacks, gourmet meals, various types of good and bad women, epigrams and epitaphs. It should be noted in passing that not a few of these topics would seem to have suggested similar Satires to Horace. In all there are preserved more than twelve hundred fragments, only a few of which consist of more than a line or two. But in some ways they are far more satisfactory than the fragments of Ennius, for they are more often cited with approval rather than to illustrate faults. It will be worthwhile to quote at some length in order to show both the cleverness and the versatility of Lucilius.

> Irritata canes quam homo quam planius dicit.
> (How much more plainly, when angry, a dog speaks than a
>   man.)

> You Albucius prefer to be called a Greek than a Roman
> Or than a Sabine. You'd be by choice a townsman of Pontus;
> You'd be a man from Tritanum, descendant of men of
>   distinction,
> Leaders and bearers of banners. And so, when you paid me
>   a visit,
> I being praetor at Athens, I greeted you as by your preference
> With the Greek "Chaere, my Titus" and all of the lictors and
>   rabble
> Hailed you in chorus with "Chaere, our Titus" and ever
>   thereafter
> You have become, Albucius, my enemy.

Another of the longer fragments also introduces Greek words into the text, a practice to be later on severely condemned by Horace and other critics.

> So you are wishing him dead whom you don't want to
>   see when you ought to.

If now this *nolueris* and *debueris* should offend you
Since, as you think, they are ἀτέχνον and, if you will have it,
Isocratean and, worse, ὀκληρῶδες altogether,
If they seem μιραχιῶδες and anything else to your fancy,
Well then, I don't give a damn.

A few of the shorter fragments offer pungent personal opinions.

He was the lesser in years. We cannot be all of us all things.

He has nor mule nor slave nor any companion whatever:
Only his purse and his money he carries about with him
        always:
Dines with his purse and sleeps with it; all his possessions
Are for the man his purse, that purse which is strapped to his
        elbow.

That was the horse, not handsome, a plodder, the best beast
        of burden.

Always he cleans the table with napkin dyed in rich purple.

Since I know well that nothing is guaranteed man
        as possession.

When she is with you alone then anything's good enough but
        when
Other men may perchance see her she decks herself out in her
        finest
Hair-do and gowns and jewelry too.

Cooks have no care if a pigtail be fair if the fat's there:
Friends consider the heart while parasites look to the money.

All that the world considers is what is your wealth and your
        status:
According to how much you have by so much you'll always
        be rated.

Two more substantial fragments come to us from Lactentius, a Christian writer of about 300 A.D. How accurately they are quoted there is no way of telling, but they have all the earmarks of genuine Lucilian origin. The first one reads:

> But nowadays from morning till night, be it holiday festive
> Or a non-holiday, all of the people and all of the fathers
> Flaunt themselves here in the forum and give themselves
>> wholly
> Unto a single interest: to cheat with caution and struggle
> Trickily and with smooth words pretend to be best of good
>> fellows.
> Meanwhile they're laying their plots as though enemies one of
>> another.

The second reads:

> Virtue, Albinus, is to have the power to value
> Properly all the affairs of life which daily concern us;
> Virtue is that a man shall value each item correctly;
> Virtue is to know what is useful, honorable, upright,
> Both what is good and what's bad, what is useless,
>> dishonorable, shameful;
> Virtue is knowing the limits to put on the search for
>> possessions;
> Virtue's ascribing to wealth no more esteem than is proper;
> Virtue is paying respect only to that which deserves it,
> To be the enemy ever of men with character evil
> And at the same time friend and defender of men that
>> are good,
> Ever to do them well and wish for them all that a friend
>> should.
> Finally, ever to hold the good of one's country in first place,
> Second the good of one's friends and, lastly only, one's own
>> good.

All these fragments show the characteristics of early Latin verse including, though not too conspicuously, alliteration (*colore, colus-*

tra; labralabellis; pectore puro; porro procedere poscent). This is so restrained as hardly to be called a vice, but Lucilius was guilty of the practice which Horace so violently denounced, the mingling of Greek words in the Latin text. I have already given the best illustration of this in citing from the fragments, but Horace's comments are worth quoting too. He makes his hypothetical defender of Lucilius say:

> But it was surely something great to introduce Greek words
> In 'mongst the Latin.

And Horace answers:

> Dunces to pedants turned, how can you so perversely
> Think it a mighty feat which even Pitholeon mastered?

But surely, answer the critics, a style made by a mixture of the two languages is pleasanter, like Chian wine mixed with Falernian, to which Horace replies ironically:

> When you are writing verses, I ask you, or when you are
>   pleading
> Difficult causes at law? I suppose when Publicola's sweating
> Or, you might say, Corvinus, on cases, you'd have him
>   commingle
> Words that he found abroad with his native ones like a
>   bilingual
> Man from Canusium?

The "fault" which no doubt seemed to Lucilius to be part of his humor did not, I suspect, seem shocking to the "singers of Euphorion."

And so we leave the early age with its pioneer strength and its bold inventions and pass on to see what effect two centuries of creative writing had on its product.

LATIN POETRY

AFTER

CHAPTER SIX

The Vigil of Venus

WITH THE *Pervigilium Veneris*, the "Vigil of Venus," we have jumped something over two hundred years from the time of Lucilius into a vastly different Rome from that of the Gracchi, Marius, and Sulla. Under the impetus given by Lucilius the expression of personal feelings and ideas in verse had become general. Furthermore, poetry was no longer a trade or a vehicle of flattery but had come to be the pursuit of free citizens of standing. It had passed through the stages of Augustan splendor and the long period of rhetoric and satire. What was to come next, marking the last period of what we call Latin literature, was suggested at the end of the first volume of this series, the romanticism of the future. The "Vigil of Venus" is an ode to spring: the goddess' festival is to take place the next day. To quote from the closing page of our second volume, "In Catullus, spring is a date—to Vergil, spring is the time for planting—to Horace, spring marks the time for congenial drinking parties in the country. But in the "Vigil of Venus" spring with all its romance bursts upon us in unrestrained passion." The gap of centuries is bridged by one curious reference to an early poet in the closing lines of the "Vigil," the mention of the tradition that "Amyclae perished through silence." The only other known reference to this tradition is to be found in Lucilius: "I must speak out for I know that Amyclae perished from silence."

The whole tone of the *Pervigilium* is set in the first line which is repeated as a refrain throughout the poem: "To-morrow he shall love who never loved and he who's loved shall love again to-morrow." The fact that spring is the real inspiration of the hymn, for hymn it is, is abruptly announced in the first stanza:

> The new spring, the singing spring: in the spring the world
>   was born;
> In the spring the loves conspire, in the spring the birds take
>   mates
> And the woods let down their tresses in the nuptial showers
>   of Spring.

But it is Venus who brings it all to pass and to-morrow, the day
of her annual festival, she will herself set up her tribunal, muster
her devotees, and issue her commands. The festival recalls to
memory the day when Venus herself was born from the union of
heaven and ocean and came sailing landward "foam borne" to
become the fountainhead of all reproduction in man and nature.

> To-morrow is the day when ether, primal ether first was wed:
> Then from moisture poured from heaven and the foam drops
>   from the sea,
> Midst the squadrons of the ocean and two-footed ocean
>   steeds
> Sprang Dione wave borne sailing under nature's nuptial
>   showers.
> To-morrow he shall love who never loved and he who's loved
>   shall love again to-morrow.

> She it is that decks the season purpling with its flowery gems;
> She it is that into clusters, underneath the West wind's breath
> Lures the swelling buds reluctant, she that sprinkles all
>   the glow
> Of the dewdrop's glittering wetness which the passing night
>   winds leave.
> To-morrow he shall love who never loved and he who's loved
>   shall love again to-morrow.

To the festival Venus has summoned the Nymphs and Cupids to
pay court to her.

> She the goddess calls the nymphs to gather in the mystic
>   grove;

With her comes her boy but think not—for it's not to be
      believed—
Cupid would bring his arrows with him when he's bent on
      festival:
Fear not, maidens, he is weaponless, he is bent on holiday.
To-morrow he shall love who never loved and he who's loved
      shall love again to-morrow.

He was bidden to leave his weapons, bidden naked to come
      forth,
Do no harm with bow and arrow or the flame of Cupid's
      torch.
None the less take heed, ye maidens, Cupid naked's passing
      fair,
All unarmed he's still all powerful, weaponless he's just
      the same.
To-morrow he shall love who never loved and he who's loved
      shall love again to-morrow.

The festival is to be in a woodland grove but the woods are tradi-
tionally the hunting ground of Diana, or as she is called here,
because of her birthplace, the maid of Delos. But the chaste Diana
is scarcely a suitable guest at such a festival and also there should
be no bloodshed connected with it. So on both grounds she is
besought to absent herself from these particular woods for the
next three nights.

Venus sends you of her following maidens chaste as you
      are chaste.
One request alone we make thee: do thou, Delian maid,
      withdraw
That the woodlands be untainted by the death of creatures
      wild
As it spreads its verdant shadows o'er the newly opened
      flowers.
To-morrow he shall love who never loved and he who's loved
      shall love again to-morrow.

> She herself would bid you welcome could she bend your
>   chastity;
> She herself would hail your presence if it became a virgin
>   maid.
> Now for three nights you'd behold these festive choirs
>   carousing here,
> Dancing through your glades amid the celebrating multitude.
> To-morrow he shall love who never loved and he that's loved
>   shall love again to-morrow.

More suitable partakers of the festivities will be Bacchus and
Ceres, the deities of wine and food, and Apollo, the god of poetry
and song, and so, with Venus as mistress of ceremonies and the
suitable gods suitably arrayed, it is for Diana to retire gracefully.
Venus shall be properly enthroned surrounded by the gay flowers
of Hybla.

> Wearing garlands made of flowers, wandering through the
>   myrtle bowers,
> Bacchus and Ceres will not fail us nor the god of poesy:
> With no rest or intermission all the night shall ring with song,
> In the woods shall reign Dione: Maid of Delos, pray retire.
> To-morrow he shall love who never loved and he who's loved
>   shall love again to-morrow.

> She, the goddess, will be seated midst the flowers of Hybla's
>   slopes;
> She herself will issue mandates with the Graces by her side.
> Hybla, pour forth all your flowers, all the flowers the year
>   sends forth;
> Hybla, don your cloak of blossoms, far as plains of Enna
>   stretch.
> To-morrow he shall love who never loved and he who's loved
>   shall love again to-morrow.

It is Venus who has been the source of the Roman race with its
combination of Trojan stock and Latin and afterwards with the

infusion of the Sabine element. Hence, through a long succession,
Venus becomes the ancestress of both Aeneas and Caesar.

> She herself, the great creatress, with her life enkindling breath
> Sways all mortal flesh and spirit with unseen omnipotence.
> She herself her Trojan offspring grafted onto Latin stock,
> Brought about the Sabine union with the sons of Romulus.
> To-morrow he shall love who never loved and he who's loved
>   shall love again to-morrow.

> She it was that to her offspring proffered the Laurentian maid,
> Presently to Mars submitted from her shrine the maiden fair.
> Thence came Ramnes and Quirites and for further issue came
> Romulus the sire and Caesar, grandchild of her noble line.
> To-morrow he shall love who never loved and he who's loved
>   shall love again to-morrow.

And so we come to the final enigmatic stanzas in sharp contrast
with each other. The one presents the happy songs of love throughout the countryside, the other the puzzling silence of the speaker
with the unsolved riddle of Amyclae's destruction through silence.

> Now the raucous swans go crashing through the silence of
>   the swamps;
> Now laments the maid of Tereus neath the lofty poplar's
>   shade,
> Till you'd think that she was sweetly singing happy songs
>   of love,
> Not a sister's grim complaining of a husband barbarous.
> To-morrow he shall love who never loved and he who's loved
>   shall love again to-morrow.

> She is singing; I am silent. When shall come for me my spring?
> When shall I be like the swallow, cease at last to voiceless be?
> I have killed the Muse by silence and Apollo casts me off.
> So Amyclae, being silent, perished by its silence mute.
> To-morrow he shall love who never loved and he who's
>   loved shall love again to-morrow.

We need not resort to the ecstasies of enthusiasm which this unique poem aroused in Mr. Mackail to admit that, whether or not we can wholly understand it, the poem awakens an emotional stir within us and that it has in it a romanticism quite out of character with our conventional conception of the practical and somewhat prosaic Roman.

CHAPTER SEVEN

Namesianus

ALL THAT WE KNOW of M. Aurelius Olympicus Namesianus is that
he came from Carthage and lived at the end of the third century
and that he wrote pastorals in imitation of Vergil, pastorals which
long passed as those of Calpurnius Siculus. He also wrote an
hexameter poem on hunting of which we possess some 325 verses.
Needless to say, the pastorals closely resemble those of Vergil, the
first eclogue beginning with Timetas speaking:

> While you are busy weaving, Tityrus, a basket
> From river rushes and the countryside is free
> From raucous voiced cicadas, sing to me some song
> That you've composed to go with slender pipes. For Pan
> Has taught you how to pipe, Apollo to make your verses.
> Begin then while the goats are grazing in the willows,
> The cows in the meadow and while the dew and gentle sun
> Persuade you to permit your flocks to roam at large.

Tityrus protests that he is too old to sing and that age has long
since cooled the passion that could inspire songs of love. Timetas
must sing for him.

> For you are young and all the country rings with praise
> Of you. Twas not so long ago, with me as judge,
> You mocked the pipes of Mopsus while old Meliboeus
> Listened with me and praised your singing to the skies.
> He has filled out the span of life, is dwelling now

In some secluded realm of heaven. So let your pipes
Sing to his spirit.

Timetas needs no more urging and when they have settled down
comfortably begins his song:

Ether, thou parent of all things and their primal cause,
Ye waters, earth, the mother of things corporeal,
And thou too, vital air, receive these songs of mine
And waft them on to Meliboeus if perchance
There be permitted feelings to souls that have passed through
                    death.

After a long tribute to Meliboeus we arrive at the conventional
ending of an eclogue:

And now the sun is driving his steeds adown the sky
And bids us drive our herds down to the river waters.

The second eclogue is of another familiar type. Two young
boys, each in turn, sing at some length to their loves without any
judge or any decision as to their relative merits but with the
conventional ending:

So sang the boys throughout the day of Donace
Until the cool of Hesperus bade them leave the woods
And lead their well-fed bulls from pasturage to stalls.

In the third eclogue two boys, Nictylus and Micon, find Pan
asleep and, filching his pipes, try to play upon them. The result
is a raucous noise which awakens Pan who consents to sing for
them the tale of Bacchus, his birth, his nurture at the hands of the
Satyrs and old Silenus, and the origin of wine, the source of song.
    In the fourth eclogue Lycidus and Mopsus sing of their respec-
tive loves in alternative five-line stanzas with a refrain closing each
stanza: "Sing each his love and soothe with song his heart's
distress."
    Such are the pastorals of Nemesianus, third rate imitations of

Vergil. His other surviving verse contribution is called *Cynogetica* or "The Chase," 325 lines and incomplete.

> I sing the thousand phases of the chase, the toils
> Delightful and its sudden dashes, battles in
> The quiet countryside. My heart is now bestirred
> By the Aonian goad. The Muses' Hill calls me
> To widespread journeys and the Castalian deity
> Offers new cups from his spring to his foster child
> And, after distant journeyings through the open country,
> Imposes yet again his yoke, entangling me
> In ivy clusters, forcing me through pathless ways
> Where are no traces of a passing wheel.

All these claims of originality cannot fail to recall similar (but more gracefully made) claims by Lucretius—"I follow the uncharted ways of the Muses untrodden before by any man's foot"—, by Vergil in the *Georgics* and by Horace—"I, priest of the Muses, sing new songs never heard before, for boys and maidens." Nemesianus next enumerates the hackneyed subjects which he will not treat. Later on, he will sing of the Emperor's great achievements, but now, with the help of the huntress goddess, he will sing of the chase. This introduction takes over a hundred lines and the lack of originality need not be pointed out.

The next 142 lines are given to the rearing and selection of hunting dogs, then sixty lines to the proper hunting horses and some sixty more to the making of nets. Finally, at line 324:

> So let us, while the morn is young, be off to hunting
> While the earth, fresh with dew, retains the tracks of beasts.

And that is as far as the fragmentary poem, "The Chase," takes us.

There are also two very questionable bits from a supposed poem on bird catching dubiously ascribed to Nemesianus.

CHAPTER EIGHT

Ausonius

DECIMUS MAGNUS AUSONIUS was born about 310 at Bordeaux. His father was Julius Ausonius, a physician. His mother was Aemilia Aeonia, half Aeduan, half Aquitanian. From her he seems for some reason to have been repelled. He was educated at Bordeaux and Toulouse and taught at Bordeaux as a *grammaticus*. About 334 he married Atturia Sabina. They had two sons, one of whom died in infancy, and one daughter. Presently he was promoted to be a *rhetor*. After thirty years of teaching at the school in Bordeaux he became the tutor of Gratian, the future Emperor. In 368–9 he accompanied Valentinian I on his campaign against the Germans. He became *comes* (count) in 370 and in 375 *quaestor*. From the end of 375, when Gratian became Emperor, his political advance became rapid. In 378 was made Praefectus Galliarum and in 379 consul. By that time he had returned to Bordeaux to take over estates left him by his father who died in 378. With Maximius' revolution Ausonius lost all prestige but was allowed to live on quietly in Bordeaux where he died in 393 or 394. He accepted Christianity in name but always remained in reality a pagan. His greatest poem, The *Moselle*, was written about 371. This is his only production which has attained lasting fame, but we cannot appreciate the literary tone (perhaps barrenness would be the better word) of the day if we do not glance at the many trifles that came from his pen.

These may well be grouped in accordance with the periods of his life during which they were written. The first period runs from 334 to 364, that is the years during which he was teaching in

Bordeaux. The earliest product of this period is found in a group of poems which he calls Epistles, addressed to his father on the occasion of the birth of a son and the formal acknowledgment of the son by Ausonius' father. It consists of twenty elegiac couplets.

> Hitherto I had believed that nothing could raise the affection
>> Wherein, my much honored father, you are enshrined in my heart.
> But there is added to-day by the grace of the gods and by virtue
>> Of this your grandson who binds us closer in union of name:
> As he is grandson to you to me he is son in the same way
>> As I am son to you, making us fathers both.

And so it continues, artificial, sentimental, and crude. Nor are the five epigrams to his wife, nor in fact any of the epigrams which seem to date from this period, of any more distinguished quality. They are the pitiful efforts of a young scribbler and show little promise of future success.

The second period, that from 364 to 383, while not the most prolific and while it contains much which is banal in the extreme, does contain the one greatest achievement of Ausonius, The *Moselle*. The "Easter Verses" were written by order of the Emperor and are obviously "commission" work. The "Griphus" discourses at length on the mystic number, three. The "Cento Nuptialis" (like the Griphus, written while he was on his campaign in Germany but published later) is inexcusably coarse in content and tone. The "Bissula" consists of six short pieces in various meters, all in honor of a captive German girl assigned to Ausonius as his share of the plunder from the German campaign. Next came the "Mosella" which will be discussed later on, and then a few minor pieces of no distinction.

The third period, from 383 down to his death ten years later contains the greatest number of items but probably only for the reason that Ausonius reserved them for publication until he had attained some standing as a poet. It may have been that his retire-

ment led to greater productivity but if so it did little to improve
the quality of the product. He wrote a short poem, "On his
Patrimony", and then the more ambitious "Fasti", a list of the
kings and consuls of Rome from the foundation of the city down
to his own consulship. It is practically all lost. A similar work
was the "Caesares", a list of the emperors from Nerva to Helio-
gababalus. Of about the same date were the "Protrepticus", an
exhortation to his grandson, and "Cupid Crucified", suggested by
a wall painting at Treves. After the death of Gratian came a period
of dejection during which he wrote nothing. Then came the
"Parentalia", a series of thirty poems mostly in elegiacs which
celebrate the memory of the poet's deceased relatives. Similarly
the "Professores" commemorates the teachers at Bordeaux. The
"Epitaph" is a series of epigrams on the heroes of the Trojan War.
The "Order of Famous Cities" is a tribute to the twenty leading
cities of the empire and finally the passion for lists peters out in
the "Technopaegnion", a list of the monosyllabic words in Latin.
The "Masque of the Seven Sages" winds up the roll of Ausonius'
works in verse.

It remains to return to The *Moselle* for a more specific study.
We have a letter from Symmachus to Ausonius asking why he has
not sent him the poem. He has read it because, he says, it has been
much circulated. "I rank it with the works of Vergil." This comment is of no critical value, but it does indicate the literary taste
of the day and the barrenness of its literary production. However,
the object of our scrutiny is to know the poem as a whole and
to understand the quality of that romanticism which made it so
full of appeal to a man like Symmachus.

The author begins abruptly, plunging *in medias res.*

> Already I had crossed the cloud-wrapped Nar
> And gazed upon the ramparts around Vincum
> Where once the Gauls produced a second Cannae
> With slaughtered hordes unburied and unwept.
> Then through a pathless forest I made my way,
> No human cultivation to be seen,
> Passing Dumnisium in an arid land
> And then Taburnae with its eternal spring

Through fields that now Sarmatian settlers hold.
At last, upon the verge of Belgic soil,
Came Noiomagen to my eager sight,
The famous camp of sainted Constantine.

As Ausonius proceeds northward he enters country which delights him because it reminds him of his own Bordeaux landscape.
At last he comes to the junction with the Moselle and bursts out
into a eulogistic address to the river itself.

Hail, river blessed by fields and husbandmen
To whom the Belgians owe their imperial pomp.
Thy hills o'ergrown with Bacchus' fragrant vines,
Thy meadows verdant with abundant grass,
Ship-bearing as the sea, sloped as a river,
Smooth as a lake with surface like to glass.
Brooks canst thou match in hurrying downward flow
And springs surpass with grateful cooling draughts.
All this is thine, what spring and brook and river
Can offer and ocean with its ebb and flow.

Then he breaks off with a more conventional depreciation of
the city home with its proverbial adornments of marble pavements
and coffered ceilings with an appreciation of the simple river shore
and its beauties.

Go now and cover your smooth floors with slabs
Of Phrygian marbles making a sheer expanse
Of overlay upon your coffered ceilings,
While I in scorn of what your wealth provides
Shall marvel rather at the work of nature,
Not in what spendthrift waste nor want desports.
Here the firm sand covers the moistened shore
Till footsteps leave no tell-tale marks behind.
Through your smooth surface you disclose your depths
And, as the pure air's open to our gaze
Nor keeps our eyes from peering through its void,
So we may see far down within your depths

The secrets hidden there beyond our reach
As softly moves the surface and your stream
Reveals the scattered forms in azure light.

He enumerates the marvels that appear to one looking down
into the clear water, the ripples in the sandy bottom, the quivering
water grasses, the plantlike seaweeds and the many colored pebbles,
to say nothing of the fish that flash hither and yon. Unhappily the
mention of fish leads Ausonius into the dreariest of digressions, a
sixty-five line catalogue of the fish of the river. It ends at last
and he returns to the more welcome account of the shores of the
river.

Now 'tis enough to have told the tale of fishes,
Their glistening hosts, their legions manifold.
Time to behold another pageant here:
The vines of Bacchus summon hence our gaze
Where the far stretching ridges lift the slopes
Of gentle hillsides rising in the sun
To make a natural theater. So the vintage,
The precious vintage, clothes the ridge of Gaunus
And Rhodope and so Lyaeus decks
His special haunt, the high Pangaean hills
And so the Ismarian slopes by Thracian sea
And even so *my* vineyards by yellow Garumna.
For from the topmost ridge to the riverside
The slopes are thickly planted with the vine.
The happy folk are busy with their toil,
Exchanging shouts in boisterous rivalry
And here some traveller on the grassy bank
Or bargeman floating by exchange rude jests
With the vine dressers till the echoes ring.
I can believe too that goat-footed satyrs
Frighten the grey eyed nymphs beneath the stream.

Ausonius lingers awhile over the scene of nymphs and satyrs
sporting in the depths and then gives himself up to a thoroughly
sentimental picture of the river at sunset when bank and river

merge and the boatman in midstream beholds the river all about
him. Then suddenly he turns to the sport of mock battle in which
the young men engage.

> And when the oared skiffs join in mimic battle
> How gay the pageant as they circle there
> And all the husbandmen upon the slope
> Forget their labor as they watch the sport
> Of happy boys leaping from bow to stern
> And present joy shuts out their dreary cares.

The mock battle recalls too many learned parallels to the mind
of the poet but he finally comes back to his account of the river
and tells of the fishermen along the bank.

> Now where the bank makes easy the approach
> Come fishermen in droves to ply their trade
> And trail their dripping nets out in midstream
> And sweep in shoals of fish caught in the mesh.
> Here one is drawing his seine buoyed up with cork
> Where thc stream flows more gently close in shore
> And yonder on the rocks still others drop
> Their lines with pliant rod and baited hook.
> The fish, deceived, swallow both bait and barb
> And soon are floundering on the sunny rocks.

We are next called upon to admire the fine houses along the
river. Worthy products, these country seats, of any of the world's
great architects who incidentally are wearisomely recalled along
with their chief monuments. After the country seats comes another
list, that of the tributaries which gladly resign their own inde-
pendence to merge with the Moselle.

> All this in sight of country seats that deck
> The hills on either bank of the flowing stream
>
> Who can describe the glories of those homes,
> Works that the flyer Daedalus would not scorn

Who built the temple at Euboean Cumae,
Nor yet great Philo who at Athens wrought
Nor Archimedes guarding Syracuse
Nor Varro's famous Seven Architects.

Such must have built these stately mansions here
In Belgic Gaul to be the river's glory.
One stands high up upon the natural rock,
One has foundations laid by the river's bank.

How can I tell of all the countless streams
That swell thy volume as thou wert the ocean?
Gladly they lose their own identity
To merge in thine; Promea, Nemesa,
And Sura, Celbis swift and Erubis,
Famed for its marbles, feeble Lesura,
Tiny Drahoma and the rivulet
Salmona. But Saravus broad that bears
Ships on his waves, no rivulet is he;
Far has he travelled neath imperial walls
To join with thee. And Alisontia,
Flowing through country rich in fruit and corn.
These and a thousand others. If to thee
Smyrna or Mantua had given a poet
Of proper stature, then would Simois
And Tiber yield to thee. Oh Rome, forgive
For Tiber guards the seat of empire and
The stately homes of Rome.

At last the poet pulls himself together, calls on the Muse to halt,
begs the Rhine to give welcome to the Moselle, identifies himself
with a brief account of his life and concludes with a final encomium
of the Moselle.

Now spread, oh Rhine, your folds caerulean
And make room for a brother stream that comes
To join with yours its waters. More than that,
It comes from the imperial town of Treves

And has beheld the triumphs of those twain,
Father and son, beyond the source of Ister,
Unknown as yet to Latin chroniclers.

Such is the tale I undertook to tell,
I of Viviscan stock yet by old ties
Of long friend-guestship well known to the Belgae.
I am Ausonius, Roman is my name
But I was born between the frontiers of
Gaul and Pyrene where gay Aquitaine
Mellows the spirits of her sons. My daring
Is greater than my genius. May it prove
No sin that I have launched upon the stream
Of poesy with this poor offering.

Horned Moselle, worthy to be renowned
Throughout all shores, not only in those wastes
Where, at your spring of origin, you show
The gilded honor of your bull-like brow
Nor only where you pass through placid fields
Nor only where you open up your course
Below the German harbors. If some praise
Should breathe upon this tenuous poem of mine,
If any man shall spend his leisure on it,
You shall ere pass upon the lips of men
And shall be cherished in a joyful song.
Thee shall I praise to all the dark blue lakes
And to the many deep voiced rivers too
And I shall praise thee to sea-like Garunna.

CHAPTER NINE

Claudian

CLAUDIUS CLAUDIANUS was born about 370, probably in Egypt. He did not visit Rome until 394. All that he wrote to that time was written in Greek. We know that he shortly moved to Milan for five years and that he was given a statue there in 402 by vote of the senate. In 404 he married a protégée of one Serena and died the same year while on his honeymoon. He was at his best in invective. His hero was Stilicho the Vandal, whose wife was Serena, the niece and adopted daughter of Theodosius. It should be noted in relation to Claudian's verses that Stilicho defeated Alaric near Elis in 397.

The poems of Claudian consist of Panegyrics, Invectives, Histories of two wars, an Epithalamion and a poem in three books on the *Rape of Proserpina*. These are all of considerable length, ranging from 200 to 600 lines. In addition, there are two collections of shorter poems, quite different from each other. The first consists of four poems ranging from twelve to forty-five lines and called "Fescennine Verses in Honor of the Marriage of the Emperor Honorius." The second consists of fifty-two poems ranging in general from two lines to a hundred. But into this collection have crept a long "Praise of Serena" and a fairly long "Battle of the Giants." For the rest, they deal with the widest range of subject: a landscape, individual people, the magnet, the spring of Aponus, a shell, Archimedes' sphere, a lobster, and so on.

There is little enough originality and no distinction in the work of Claudian. The opening lines of the panegyric on the consulship of Probinus and Olybrius will serve to illustrate that branch of his persistent activity.

Sun that doth earth encircle with reins that are ever afire,
Rolling the centuries on with inexhaustible motion,
Scatter thy light with kindly beam and suffer thy coursers,
After their manes are combed while they breathe forth roseate
    fire flames,
In a more jocund mood to make the ascent of the heavens.
Now let the year bend its way for these brothers who join in
    a common
Consulship. So let the months assume a happy beginning.
Well dost thou know the Auchinian race and to thee are
    familiar
All of the Auniadae and their power for oft hast thou started
Off on thy annual cruise with their consulship for a beginning,
Setting the tone for the months to happiness following after.

The category of invective may be illustrated from the *First Book
Against Rufinus.*

Dire Allecto once, by the goad of jealousy kindled,
Seeing the cities of men far and wide at peace with each other,
Straightway summoned her hideous council of sisters infernal.
In her foul palace they gather, that numberless offspring
    begotten
Once in an evil time by Night: comes Discord, the nurse of
    battle,
Hunger imperious, Age that is kin to Death and with her
Loathesome Disease whose life is a constant burden and Envy,
Envy that cannot endure another's prosperity, Sorrow,
Coming with garments rent and Fear and foolhardy Rashness,
Sightless of eye and Luxury, ruthless destroyer of riches,
Close to whose side ever clings unhappy Poverty meekly,
All the long troop of Cares that cluster 'round Avarice,
    their brother.
Filled are the seats of iron with this foul rout of the Furies,
Filled is the chamber grim with the throng of horrible
    monsters.

The *War Against Gildo* commemorated a revolt in Africa important only in that it offered a threat to the Roman corn supply. In translating I have used the English pentameter as being better suited to active narrative than the hexameter.

> The kingdom of the south is to our empire
> Once more restored. That hemisphere subjected,
> Europe and Libya we have joined together
> Under one common lord to live like brothers.
> He who aspired to be a third to rule the empire
> Him has Honorius' son with mighty prowess
> Brought to his knees, the only triumph glorious
> Failing to grace the armies of the father.
> Ere on the coast the army had made landing
> Making no show of battle, Gildo surrendered.
> News of the victory came before war's announcement.

And yet Claudian fills 526 lines of narrative without finishing his poem. A few selections must serve to suggest the scope and quality of the shorter poems and the preface will suffice for the *Rape of Proserpina.*

Fescennine Verses III

> Stilicho, come twine with a garland soft
> The locks that are used to the helmet harsh.
> Let the trumpets cease and the marriage torch
> Banish Mars the cruel from this abode.
> Let the royal blood be mingled again
> With royal blood. With your powerful hand
> Do a father's office: make these children one.
> As Emperor's daughter you took to wife,
> Your daughter shall marry an Emperor's self.
> What place is here for jealousy mad?
> What excuse for envy is offered here?
> For Stilicho's father to both bride and groom.

On the Tomb of a Beauty

Fate to the fair denies to survive long span of life.
    Suddenly fall the great. Crumbles the highest first.
Here lies a woman fair who possessed the figure of Venus.
    Beauty so great but earned envy of gods above.

On Receiving a Gift of Honey

Sweet are the gifts you are sending me, Maximus, ever:
    Yet whatever you sent, that would be honey to me.

On Theodore and Hadrian

Manlius revels in sleep through nights and days of inertia;
    Pharius, sleepless still, steals from both gods and men.
People of Italy, let every prayer that you utter be this:
    Never may Manlius sleep, never may Pharius wake.

Preface to *Rape of Proserpina*

He who first builded a ship and ventured out on the ocean,
    Troubling the watery ways beaten by rough hewn oars,
He who first dared to commit his bark to the dubious breezes,
    Who by his art devised ways that nature denied,
First with a trembling heart tried only the tranquil waters,
    Hugging the sheltering shore, daring no distant voyage.
Presently growing bolder he sailed across wider stretches,
    Daring to leave behind coastline and continent.
Then as his courage rose he began to spread sail to the
        south wind,
    Courage turning to rash boldness with each new attempt.
Now far and wide he courses at will with the heavens to
        guide him:
    Challenges wintry cold o'er the Ionian Sea.

CHAPTER TEN

Avianus

AVIANUS SEEMS (it is very doubtful) to have lived about 400
A.D. We have forty-two of his fables. They follow principally
Babrius, the Greek, although Avianus mentions also Phaedrus.
The fables are wholly undistinguished as a few examples will amply
indicate.

The Nurse and the Child

Once on a time a nurse had sworn to her wailing infant
    If he did not keep still, he would be tossed to a wolf.
Credulous at these words a listening wolf near the cottage
    Waited expectant there, nursing his hopes in vain.
For, being weary at last, the child had dropped into slumber,
    Robbing the hungry wolf, waiting in frustrated hope.
Him when he came back home to his lair in his native forest
    Thus did his wife address, seeing her famished mate:
"Why do you come without bringing along your usual
        plunder?
    Why so haggard and drawn? Why so forlornly thin?"
"Not to deceive you" he said, "I was fooled by a trick
        malignant,
    Hardly escaped by flight, leaving the plunder behind.
As for the plunder you ask for, what hope was mine for
        plunder,
    Fooled by a scolding nurse, tricked by her empty
        threats?"

Let any man who falls for the protestations of woman
　　Take to his heart this tale: spoken for him are my words.

The Bald Horseman

Bald of pate, a horseman used once to cover his head with
　　Ringlets and in false locks hide his denuded crown.
Riding one day, full armed, over the Campus Martius,
　　Guiding responsive horse, gaily with easy rein,
Blasts from the north of Boreas meeting him squarely
　　Made him a figure of fun: bald pate exposed to view.
Quickly his wig blew off exposing a shiny forehead
　　Different in hue from what, only a moment before,
It had presented. At once with his quickness of mind he
　　　　shouted:
　　"What seems so strange to you that my adopted locks
Flee me so readily now when my own have even more quickly
　　Once in the days of old taken regretted flight?"

The Leopard and the Fox

Marked with his dappled hide, fine breasted, a leopard
　　Went to parade himself unto his fellow beasts
And since the haughty lions were lacking in mottled torsos
　　Straightway he looked with scorn on the inferior tribe.
All of the others as well with arrogant looks he derided,
　　Taking himself as the sole acme of noble mien.
While he was strutting thus in youth's inconsiderate glory
　　Up spake a fox and exposed vanity at its real worth:
"Go now" he said "and put all your trust in your childish
　　　　regalia
　　Long as you let me surpass you by the strength of
　　　　my wit,
Long as we still may admire the traits of an intellect gifted
　　Rather than those that expose merely a bodily charm."

CHAPTER ELEVEN

Namatianus

CLAUDIUS RUTILIUS NAMATIANUS came of a Gallo-Roman family, probably of Toulouse, and lived late in the fourth century. All we have of his literary output is the long fragment of a narrative poem (Book I, and sixty-eight lines of Book II) recounting his voyage home from Rome to Toulouse along the coast. The opening words indicate that the beginning of the poem is lost. In our fragment Namatianus gets only as far as Luna and the digressions are of greater interest than the narrative proper—an encomium of Rome, a description of Italy, tirades against the Jews and against Stilicho, the iron mines of Ilva and the salt pans of Vada, and so on. The poem is written in elegiac couplets. There is some virtue in the digressions but it is impossible to believe that the narrative is not an unsuccessful imitation of The *Moselle* of Ausonius. A very few bits of translation will be sufficient to illustrate the point.

The Voyage

> Rather you'll be surprised, my reader, to learn of my speedy
> Leaving of all the charms offered to man by Rome.
> Nothing can be too long for one who would sing her praises,
> Nothing too long for him, singing what all men crave.
> Oh, how greatly, how often can I count you blessed forever
> Who have deserved to be born here on this blessed soil,
> You who are nobly born of ancestors Roman, crowning
> Honorable birth with the fame lent by eternal Rome.
> No other land can there be where more fittingly heaven could
> scatter

Seeds of all virtues known, virtues yours by your birth.

Iron Mines of Ilva

Fronting our course lies Ilva with her mines of iron.
　　Noricum has produced no richer yield than hers
Nor Bitnerix though huge to behold her fabulous smelters,
　　Not the Sardinian ore pouring in molten mass.
Greater by far is the benefit wrought for the world by iron
　　Than what that gravel bestows, gold laden down Tagus'
　　　　flood.
Gold is the mother of vice and a mother prolific and vicious;
　　Blind love of gold creates every most impious act;
Golden the gifts that betray the troth of newly wed maidens;
　　Showers of gold can seduce quickly her fondest embrace;
Loyalty sapped by gold has often betrayed strong cities;
　　Scandalous misuse of gold leads to misguided ambition.
Not so with iron for with iron neglected fields are recovered;
　　Iron it was that first taught ways of civilized life.

The Mountains of Italy

The central mountains slope toward two quite separate oceans,
　　Eastward Dalmatia's sea, westward the Tuscan Sea.
So if we think that a god designed earth's marvellous fabric
　　Then were the Apennines made as a protective fringe
Woven to give us a barrier able to cover our outposts,
　　Barrier scarce to be traversed, crossed by no mountain
　　　　trails.
Nature that knew what jealousy Italy some day would gender
　　Thought the Alps slight defense gainst an approach
　　　　from the north.

CHAPTER TWELVE

Sidonius

GAIUS SOLLIUS APOLLINARIS SIDONIUS was born at Lyons about 430. His family was a distinguished one in Gaul. Sidonius received a superficial education probably at Lyons. He married Papianilla, the daughter of Avitus, by whom he had one son and three daughters. Through his connection with Avitus he became involved in this man's revolt in 455. Sidonius' grandfather had accepted Christianity and the family always remained Christian. It is not wholly strange therefore that, after a long series of crises, Sidonius abandoned the political arena to become Bishop of the Arverni at Clermont. In 475 Rome ceded the Auvergne to the Goths and Sidonius was shortly after imprisoned at Carcasonne. He was finally released and returned to Clermont, where he died about 479. We are particularly well-informed about Sidonius because many of his letters are preserved and published with his poems.

Sidonius published his poems, with a single exception, in a small volume with a proem and an envoy. The exception was a panegyric on the second consulship of the Emperor Anthemius in 468. Since Sidonius' family on both sides was distinguished there is not necessarily any ulterior motive in thus addressing the Emperor on the part of a "youth" of thirty-eight.

Panegyric to Emperor Anthemius

When in the course of time old Nature placed Jupiter firmly
High o'er the stars and he entered upon his new

Sovereign reign, then all of the gods vied madly to pay their
 Worship to their new lord, bowing to him with "Hail."
Mars with the trumpet's blare bade welcome his sire,
  proclaiming
Loudly with thunderous din, praising his thunderbolts;
Mercury, god Arcadian, joined with Apollo who sounded
 Boldly the clanging strings, Mercury strumming the lyre.
Then Castalia's band of maidens gave forth their plaudits,
 Homage of song and dance, music of reed and voice.
After the dwellers of heaven the god is said to have listened
 Patiently unto the songs demigods shouted, less sweet.
Then came the Fauns and the Dryads, the Satyrs and
  followers of Bacchus
Came in a rustic throng, singing a charming song.
Pans with their hemlock reeds deserted Maenalian heights:
 After the notes of the lyre hoarser notes tickled
  Jove's ears.
Chiron came among these and danced to the music of quills,
 Gracefully moving his hooves never yet trained to dance.
So did the half-man earn a respectful hearing and found
 Grace though he loudly neighed even the while he sang.

Here as elsewhere throughout Sidonius' poems can be caught
a graceless echo of the great poets of old (in this case of Catullus,
elsewhere of Vergil). His education had been superficial and in
his desire to exhibit his slight learning he in fact exhibits his
deficiency.

The book of poems which follows this panegyric shows a wide
variety of subject and an even wider variety in the length of the
individual poems, from four lines to more than six hundred. The
subjects include a number of panegyrics or what amount to panegyrics, two epithalamia, letters to friends, notably a letter of thanks
to Bishop Faustus, the baths of his summer estate, his swimming
pool, a fish caught at night, all embraced between a proem and an
envoy. The former has a rather clumsy reference to Vergil and a
vague suggestion of Catullus' neat dedication of *his* little volume
to Cornelius Nepos, the latter a similar suggestion of Martial. A
few examples of the poems will suffice.

On Fish Caught at Night

For the first time I caught four fishes in one night.
  Two I have kept myself, two I am sending you.
Yours are the largest which is wholly proper too
  For of my heart by far yours is the larger share.

On His Swimming Bath

Enter the chilling waves after the steaming bath.
  Let the cool water refresh that heated skin of yours.
Though it be only water with no stronger liquor therein
  Still one plunge in my bath sets your eyes swimming
    adrift.

To Ecdicius, his Brother-in-law

Birthday of mine reminds me the Nones of November are
    coming.
  Hither I do not invite: order's the word I use.
Bring too your wife with you for this time you're only two:
  Next year I hope you'll be three that will visit me.

Thanksgiving to Bishop Faustus

Thrust far from thee now, my lyre, the songs of Apollo,
Songs of the Muses nine and Pallas, the tenth of their chorus:
Orpheus too and the fabled stream of the horse's springlet.
Thrust far from thee the Theban lute that lured stones to
    follow,
Raising the listening walls. For thee 'tis more seemly to sing of
Him, your high priest, oh great spirit, that once did enter
    the heart of
Miriam long ago when Israel, seizing their timbrels,
Marched dry shod through the trough of the Red Sea waters
    suspended,
Passed through the midst of the waves, gladly acclaiming thy
    triumph.

Who was it aided the hand of Judith that smote Holophernes
Then when the prostrate trunk was laid and the throat was
    cut through,
One mighty blow had gloriously disguised the feminine
    weakness.

Envoy to His Book

Go little book and, passing out my doorway,
Never fail to remember what I tell you.
Follow the route I bid you and 'twill lead you
To my friends whose names I have duly noted.
Do not follow the ancient highway where the
Milestones mark all clearly the name of Caesar:
Make your way by easy stages and slowly:
So you'll call forth quick affection and welcome.
First of all, you'll enter Domitius' homestead,
Stern Domitius who'll cause my muse to tremble;
Surely not so stern a critic as he is
Was the man who laughed but once in his lifetime.
Yet you gladly may face his stern demeanor
For if *he* approves, you'll be hailed by all men.

Epilogue

With Sidonius ends what may properly be called "Latin Poetry." It is true that much verse has been written in Latin, from the early church hymns to contemporary Oxford effusions, good, bad, and indifferent. It is true that into the late writers whom we have been considering there had already intruded an element of Christian sanctimony. Sidonius was himself a bishop, but one cannot fail to note that throughout his pedantic versifying the music of Apollo sounds more authentic than the song of Miriam.

In our three volumes we have attempted to follow, without too much burden of scholarship, the course of Roman poetry from its composite source in Greek literature and native ballads and ritual through a period of popular comedy, unpopular tragedy, and subsidized epic; thence, by way of Lucilius, to the personal poetry of the "New Poets" and the peak achievement of the Augustans; next, through the age of rhetoric and satire to the dawning romanticism of the second and following centuries and the twilight of Latin Poetry before the fall of Rome under the assaults of Christianity and barbarian invasion.

APPENDIX

The Menaechmi of Plautus

Cast of Characters

Pen. Peniculus, a parasite
Men. 1. Menaechmus, a young gentleman of Epidamnus
Men. 2. Menaechmus, a young gentleman of Syracuse
Ero. Erotium, a courtesan
Cyl. Cylindrus, her cook
Mes. Messenio, a slave of Menaechmus of Syracuse
Maid servant of Erotium
Wife of Menaechmus of Epidamnus
Old man, father-in-law of Menaechmus of Epidamnus
Doctor, a citizen of Epidamnus

Scene: A street in Epidamnus

The *Menaechmi* was not only one of the popular plays of Plautus, but derives a particular interest for us from its modern adaptation, George Abbot's, *The Boys of Syracuse.*

Act I. Scene 1.

Pen.   The young men of the town call me Peniculus
        Because, whene'er I eat, I wipe the table clean.
        Men who put chains on captives or restrain with bonds
        Their runaway slaves in my opinion are sheer fools.
        For if new evils fall on wretched men they are
        Still more inclined to villainous acts and flight
        And they will somehow manage to break loose the door
        Or cleverly filch the key: that's nonsense all of it.
        But if you want to keep a fellow safely bound
        You ought to keep him bound with ample food and drink.
        So you should keep his mouth bound to a table full.
        For while you give him all he wants to eat and drink
        As he would have it just exactly day by day
        He'll never try to run away from you although
        He has committed capital offence. You'll surely
        Keep him securely while you bind him with such chains.
        For foodstuffs are the kind of chains that all the more
        You loosen them, the more securely do they bind.
        Now I am going to Menaechmus, for to him
        I have been sentenced. Gladly I go then to be chained,
        For that man does not merely feed: he nourishes
        And builds you up. His medicine is the very best
        For he himself, this youth, is a mighty trencherman.
        Banquets he gives quite fit for Ceres, piles the table
        With plates and platters till you're really forced to stand
        Upon the couch to reach what's on the topmost plate.
        But there has been an interval of many days
        That I've been housed at home with all my dearest
        (There's nothing that I buy or eat I count not dearest)
        And all those dearest to me are deserting me.
        So now I'm off to visit him. But look: the door
        Is opening and I see Menaechmus coming out.

Act I. Scene 2.

Men. 1. If you are not a wicked fool, without control,
         Out of your mind, to want to seem so odious
         To your own husband, then go hate yourself instead.
         And more, if you act so to me after today
         I'll send you back without a husband to your father.
         As often as I want to leave you hinder me,
         You call me back, you ask me where I'm going, what
         My business, what I am after, what I'm going
         To do. I've married a customs guard, that I must tell
         What I have been at and what I am doing next.
         I've been too soft with you. So now I'll tell you this:
         Since I provide you maids and food and wool and gold,
         Provide you with fine clothes and you still lack for nothing,
         If you have sense you will keep out of trouble and stop
         Watching your husband. More than that, that all your spying
         Be not in vain, to pay you for your nosy spying
         I'll get me a harlot and I'll take her out to dine.

Pen.   *aside* The man believes he's injuring his wife in this:
         It's really me for if he dines abroad it's me
         And not his wife that he is taking vengeance on.

Men. 1. Hurrah, at last, by Hercules, I've driven her in.
         Step up, you husbands that have lovers. Give me now
         Your gifts and your congratulations. I have battled well.
         I've stolen this cloak from her my wife to give to my love.
         That is the way to fool a nosy, prying watch dog.
         Fine job, neat trick, good show and mighty neatly done.
         At my own cost I've robbed an evil woman to take
         The plunder to my own chief plunderer. I've taken
         Good booty from the foe to help my own allies.

Pen.   Hey there, young man, is some part of that booty mine?

Men. 1. I'm lost. I've fallen into ambush.

Pen.   Nay, into safety.

Men. 1. Who's that?

Pen.   It's me.

Men. 1.   Oh joy, what opportunity.

Hail!

Pen.   Hail!

Men. 1.   What say?

Pen.   I hold my Genius by the hand.

Men. 1. You couldn't have come more opportunely than you do.

Pen.   That is my wont. I know all tricks of helping out.

Men. 1. Would'st see a luscious concoction?

Pen.   Who's the cook that cooked it?
I'll know if he blundered when I taste what's left of it.

Men. 1. Tell me, have you ever seen a painting on the wall
Where an eagle carried off Catameitus or Venus Adonis?

Pen.   Often, but what is that to me?

Men. 1.   Come, look at me.
Do I resemble it at all?

Pen.   What's that you're wearing?

Men. 1. Tell me I am a charming figure.

Pen.   Where are we eating?

Men. 1. Just tell me what I bade you.

Pen.   All right then: you're charming.

Men. 1. Can't you add anything?

Pen.   And also entertaining.

Men. 1. Go on.

Pen.   I'll not go on until I know what's in it.
You've quarrelled with your wife, so I am on my guard.

Men. 1. Without her knowing, let's find a place to burn up the day.

Pen.   Come, that sounds fair. I'll light the pyre as quick as a wink:
The day's already at least half dead, down to the navel.

Men. 1. You are delaying yourself abusing me.

Pen.   Knock out
My one good eye if I speak aught but what you order.

Men. 1. Come here away from the door.

Pen.   All right.

Men. 1.   No, further.

Pen.   Well?

Men. 1. Come bravely hither towards me from that lion's lair.

Pen.   By Pollux, I think you'd make a splendid horse race driver.

Men. 1. How so?

Pen.   You keep a backward glance to see if she follows.
Men. 1. What say you?
Pen.   I? Just what you wish, or yes or no.
Men. 1. Can you conjecture anything from smell if you
        But get a whiff?
Pen.   You'd better get the board of augurs.
Men. 1. Come smell the cloak. What does it suggest to you? You balk?
Pen.   One ought to smell the upper part of a woman's cloak.
        From that part there an unwashable stench defiles the nose.
Men.   Well, smell it here. How very fastidious!
Pen.   Yes, 'tis seemly.
Men. 1. Well then, what smell you?
Pen.   Theft, adultery, a dinner.
Men. 1. I'll give it to the courtesan here, Erotium,
        And bid her make a dinner for me and you and her.
        Then we will revel till the morning star appears.
Pen.   That's a fine tale you tell. Shall I then knock?
Men. 1.   Yes, knock.
        Or wait—
Pen.   You've shoved the drinking bowl a mile away.
Men. 1. Knock softly.
Pen.   You're afraid the door is crockery?
Men. 1. Wait! Wait! She's coming out.
Pen.   Look at the sun:
        Its brightness is obscured by all this splendid sheen.

Act I. Scene 3.

Ero.   My love, Menaechmus, hail!
Pen.   And me?
Ero.   You do not count.
Pen.   The fate of all auxiliaries to the legion, always.
Men. 1. I've ordered I should have a battle here today.
Ero.   So it shall be.
Men. 1.   And then we'll have a drinking bout
        To see who's found the best man at the drinking bowl.

	The general, you. You choose with which you spend the night.
	How I do hate my wife when I see you, my darling.
Ero.	And yet you can't but put on something that is hers.
	What's that?
Men. 1.	Taken from her to put on you, my rose.
Ero.	How easily you outstrip all those that seek my favor!
Pen.	*aside* A harlot flatters only when she sees some plunder.
	For if she loved him truly, she'd have bitten his nose off.
Men. 1.	Hold this, Peniculus. I want to present the plunder.
Pen.	Give it me: but I beg you later, dance in the palla.
Men. 1.	I dance? You're mad, by Hercules.
Pen.	I mad—or you?
	If you won't dance then take it off.
Men. 1.	I won this booty
	At mighty risk. Not Hercules himself I think
	Stole at such risk the girdle of Hippolyta.
	Take it: you are the only girl that just suits me.
Ero.	And so compatible should true lovers ever be.
Pen.	Who plunge on headlong into abject poverty.
Men. 1.	I paid four minae for that cloak to give my wife.
Pen.	To balance the account: four minae gone to the devil.
Men. 1.	You know what I would have arranged?
Ero.	I know: I'll do it.
Men. 1.	Then have a good rich meal prepared for three of us
	And get some special delicacies from the forum:
	Pigs' knuckles, special ham and luscious pigs' brains too
	And any other dainty you can conjure up.
	Have it all steaming hot and piled on the table
	And straightaway.
Ero.	By Castor, yes.
Men. 1.	We're for the forum.
	We'll be back presently to drink while things are cooking.
Ero.	Come when you will. All will be ready.
Men. 1.	Hurry up then.
	And you, come follow me.
Pen.	By Hercules, I'll do that.
	'Twould take the wealth of all the gods to make me lose you.
Ero.	Summon the cook Cylindrus now to me at once.

Act I. Scene 4.

Ero. You take your basket and some money—here are three guineas.
Cyl. I've got them.
Ero.   Go and buy the dinner, enough for three.
Enough, be sure, but not too much.
Cyl.   What sort of folk?
Ero. Myself, Menaechmus, and his parasite.
Cyl.   That's ten.
That parasite can easily perform for eight.
Ero. I've named the guests: the rest is your affair.
Cyl.   All right,
It's done. Bid them sit down.
Ero.   Be quick.
Cyl.   I'll be here shortly.

Act II. Scene 1.

Men. 2. There is I think, Messenio, no greater pleasure
For sailors than the moment when, from out at sea,
They catch a glimpse of land.
Mes.   Still greater, I maintain,
If they behold on landing earth that has been theirs.
But why, I ask you, have we come to Epidamnus,
Or do we, like the sea, go sailing round all islands?
Men. 2. Ay, ay, 'tis so—to search for that twin brother mine.
Mes. Well then, what limit to that endless search for him?
It's now the sixth year that we've been on this affair.
The Istrian Sea, the Spanish, the Massilian,
Illyrian too, the northern sea, the exotic Greek,
And all the Italian shore the wide, wide seas can reach.
We've sailed them all. I'm sure if you were looking for
A needle you'd have found it long ago if truly
There was one. But you seek the dead amongst the living.
We should have found him long ago if he were living.
Men. 2. If so, then I must find someone to make it certain,

Who says he knows for very fact that he is dead.
That known, I'll waste no more my time on searching him.
But else, so long as I shall live, I will not cease,
For I alone know this, how dear he is to me.

Mes.   You're looking for a knot in a rush. Why don't we now
Go home at once—unless you plan to write a novel.

Men. 2.   Do what you're told, eat what you're given, keep out of trouble
And don't annoy me. It's no concern of yours.

Mes.   *aside*   Aha!
With that word I know well that I am but a slave.
But none the less I cannot keep myself from speaking.
aloud Listen, Menaechmus, when I look into our purse
By Hercules, there's nothing there but summer rations.
And so, by Hercules, unless you'll go back home
When you have nothing left at all, you'll groan for it.
These men of Epidamnus are not known for kindness.
They are gross voluptuaries and mighty drinkers too
And sycophants and sponges to the last degree
That live here in this city—yes and courtesans—
Nowhere in the world they say are men more plausible.
That's how the city got the name of Epidamnus:
Because that no one visits here without great harm.

Men. 2.   I'll be on guard against all that.   Give me the purse.

Mes.   Why do you want it?

Men. 2.   I'm afraid from what you say.

Mes.   Afraid of what?

Men. 2.   That you harm me in Epidamnus.
For you, Messenio, are a great one for the ladies,
But I'm a man of temper with a reckless wrath.
So I will guard against both things if I've the purse:
You'll not go wrong nor shall I lose my temper at you.

Mes.   Take it and keep it—that will give me greatest pleasure.

Act II.   Scene 2.

Cyl.   I've purchased well the dainties. After my own heart

I'll spread a goodly feast here for these banqueters.
But look, I see Menaechmus. Oh, my back, my back!
The banqueters already come walking to the door
Before I've spread the feast. I'll have to speak to them.
Menaechmus, hail.

Men. 2.   God bless you. Know you who I am?

Cyl.   Of course, by Hercules. Where are the other guests?

Men. 2.   What other guests look you for?

Cyl.   Where is your parasite?

Men. 2.   My parasite? The man has certainly gone mad.

Mes.   Didn't I tell you the place was full of sycophants?

Men. 2.   Young man, who is this parasite of mine you want?

Cyl.   Peniculus.

Men. 2.   But look, it's safe here in my pack.

Cyl.   See here, Menaechmus, you've come on the dot for dinner.
I'm just back from the shopping

Men. 2.   Come now, answer me,
Young man. How much do pigs cost, unpolluted pigs,
Ready for sacrifice?

Cyl.   A dollar.

Men. 2.   Well, take it from me
And get yourself well exorcised at my expense.
For I am thoroughly convinced that you are crazy,
Whoever you are, to pester me, a stranger here.

Cyl.   I am Cylindrus. Don't you know me by that name?

Men. 2.   Cylindrus then, or Coliendrus, may you perish.
I neither know you now nor ever wish to know you.

Cyl.   Just tell me this (what I am sure of) are you Menaechmus?

Men. 2.   You talk like a sane man when you call me by my name.
But when did you know me?

Cyl.   When, you ask, did I know you
Who have my mistress her Erotium, for your sweetheart?

Men. 2.   I certainly have not nor do I know who you are.

Cyl.   You don't know who I am who have so often here
Poured out the drinks when you have come to revel?

Mes.   My god!
That I have nothing here to smash the man's head with!

Men. 2. You often poured me drinks—me who until this day
         Have never seen Epidamnus?
Cyl.   You deny it all?
Men. 2. By Hercules, I do.
Cyl.   But isn't that house there
         Your house?
Men. 2.   I pray the gods destroy all that live there.
Cyl.   The man is surely crazy so to curse himself.
         Look here, Menaechmus.
Men. 2.   Well?
Cyl.   If you'd take my advice,
         You'd take that dollar that you offered me just now
         And, if you've any sense, get for yourself a pig.
         For surely you, by Hercules, are the crazy one,
         Menaechmus, when you call down curses on yourself.
Mes.   By Hercules, this man disgusts me heartily.
Cyl.   He often jollies me as a joke in just that fashion.
         He can be quite ridiculous when his wife's not here.
Men. 2. What's that you say?
Cyl.   Is this enough that you see here?
         What I have brought for the three of you? Have I bought enough
         For you, your parasite, and the woman?
Men. 2.   What woman, man,
         What parasite are you talking of?
Mes.   What can possess you
         To pester the man?
Cyl.   What have I got to do with you?
         I don't know you—I'm talking with this man I know.
Men. 2. By Pollux, the man is crazy, I am sure of that.
Cyl.   I'll see that these are cooked at once without delay.
         Don't you go wandering off too far from our house here.
         Anything more?
Men. 2.   Yes this, that you go straight to hell.
Cyl.   It's better, by Hercules, that you come in and rest.
         While I submit this food to Vulcan's violence.
         I'll go right in and tell Erotium you're here
         That she may take you off and not keep standing here.

Men. 2. Has he really gone? Those words then which you spoke before
        They were no lies.
Mes.   You just watch out then for yourself.
        For I believe that courtesan lives in this house,
        The crazy man was telling about who just left us.
Men. 2. I wonder all the same how he came to know my name.
Mes.   That's no great marvel. 'Tis the way with courtesans
        To send their slaves and maidens to the harborside
        If any foreign ship perchance may come to port.
        They find out whose it is and what his name may be
        And then they fasten on him, stick to him like glue.
        And if they've once enticed him, send him home despoiled.
        Now in *this* port before us rides a pirate ship
        From which we'd better keep well away—that's my advice.
Men. 2. By Hercules, that's good advice.
Mes.   Well, I'll be sure
        That I have counselled well if you watch out as well.
Men. 2. Be silent for a bit. The door begins to creak.
        Let's watch who's coming out.
Mes.   Meanwhile I'll rest this pack.
        Here now, you sailors, watch this luggage here. Be sharp.

Act II. Scene 3.

Ero.   Now, leave the door like that. I do not wish to have it shut.
        Get ready all within. See to it that all is done
        That need be. Spread the couches well and light the incense.
        All charming niceties delight the hearts of lovers.
        Perfection is the ruin of lovers but my gain.
        But where's the man cook said was standing here outside?
        There: look, I see him, who's going to be my game and also
        My greatest source of profit, who on his part as well
        Deserves to be the most welcome guest here in my house.
        I will approach him and I'll be the first to speak.
        Oh, darling of my soul, I cannot understand
        Why you are standing here outside the while the door

	Is open to you wider than the door of your
	Own house. It is your house and all is ready for you
	Just as you ordered, as you wished. And now for you
	There is no reason to delay. The meal you ordered
	Is all prepared. So when you will come in, recline.
Men. 2.	Who is she talking to?
Ero.	With you, of course.
Men. 2.	But what
	Have I ever had to do with you?
Ero.	Why, that 'tis you
	That Venus bids me honor and you well deserve it,
	For by your benefactions you have made me flourish.
Men. 2.	But she is crazy too or drunk, Messenio,
	To address a total stranger in such endearing terms.
Mes.	Didn't I tell you this would happen? So far the leaves
	Are falling on you. After three days the trees will fall.
	For such the ways of greedy harlots to entice men.
	But let me talk. Hey, woman, I'm speaking to you.
Ero.	Well?
Mes.	Where have you known this man?
Ero.	Where he has long known me,
	In Epidamnus.
Mes.	What! In Epidamnus, where
	He's not set foot until today?
Ero.	Menaechmus,
	You're making sport of me. But come inside—it's better.
Men. 2.	By Pollux, this woman calls me by my proper name.
	I wonder what she's up do.
Mes.	Oh, she smells the purse
	That you've got there.
Men. 2.	By Pollux, you remind me well:
	You take it. I'll see whether she loves me or the purse.
Ero.	Come, let's go in and dine.
Men. 2.	You're very kind but thanks.
Ero.	Then why, pray, did you bid me get the dinner ready?
Men. 2.	I bade you?
Ero.	Surely you did—for you and your parasite.

Men. 2. What in the devil's name: my parasite. She's mad.
Ero.   Peniculus.
Men. 2.   Who's this Peniculus? A wash cloth?
Ero.   The man that came with you a while ago when you
         Brought me the cloak you'd stolen from your wife.
Men. 2.   What's that?
         I gave you a cloak I'd stolen from my wife? Are you sane?
         This woman like a horse is dreaming standing up.
Ero.   Why do you want to mock me and keep on denying
         What you have done?
Men. 2.   Say what I've done that I deny.
Ero.   Today you gave me your wife's cloak.
Men. 2.   I still deny it.
         I have no wife and never had one and I never
         Since I was born set foot within this harbor town.
         I ate aboard, I came ashore, I met you.
Ero.   Look here,
         I'm lost. What is that boat you talk about?
Men. 2.   Of wood,
         Well worn and often mended, beaten by the mallet.
         As when one stretches hides, each peg lies close to peg.
Ero.   I beg you, please stop teasing: come with me inside.
Men. 2. Woman, it is some other man you want, not me.
Ero.   Don't I then know Menaechmus, grandson he of Moschus?
         Born, so they say, in Syracuse in Sicily
         Where reigned Agathocles and later Phintia
         When Liparo who left the realm to Hiero.
         Now Hiero's king.
Men. 2.   Not false your tale.
Mes.   By Jupiter!
         She doesn't come from there to know your tale so well?
Men. 2. By Hercules, it seems so. I must go in.
Mes.   Don't do it.
         You're lost if you go in that door.
Men. 2.   You shut your mouth.
         The affair goes well. I'll agree to anything she says
         If I get entertainment. Woman, all this time

I've been with purpose crossing you. I feared this man,
That he might tell my wife about the cloak and feast.
Now, as you wish, let's in.

Ero.   By Castor, that just suits me too.
But do you know what I should like?

Men. 2.   Just order me.

Ero.   That cloak you gave me, will you take it to the dyer
To have it dyed and changes made to suit my taste?

Men. 2. By Hercules, how clever—so it can't be recognised.
My wife won't know you've got it if she comes across you.

Ero.   Then take it with you when you go.

Men. 2.   Yes, by all means.

Ero.   Then let's go in.

Men. 2.   I'll follow: I want to speak to this man.
Hey, there, Messenio, come here.

Mes.   What now?

Men. 2.   You'd know?

Mes.   What then?

Men. 2.   I need—

Mes.   Need what?

Men. 2.   You'd say how clever I am.
I've got the plunder, I've begun the job. Be off
As fast as possible. Take these men off to some joint
And come again to meet me here before the sun sets.

Mes.   Don't you yet know those houris, Master?

Men. 2.   Shut your mouth.
'Twill be my loss not yours if I should play the fool.
This woman's a stupid idiot. I've already found
There's booty for us.

Mes.   I'm lost.

Men. 2.   Be off.

Mes.   I'm lost indeed:
The pirate ship is carrying off our little skiff.
But I'm a stupid fool to try to control my master.
He bought me to take orders, not to be commander.
So I must follow as he orders. I'll meet him later.

Act III. Scene 1.

Pen.   I'm more than thirty years of age and all that time
I've never done anything worse or even criminal
Than I have done today by joining that assembly.
For while I stood agape Menaechmus slipped away
And went to his mistress I suppose nor took me with him.
May all the gods destroy the man who first conceived
Assemblies, to keep busy men like me confined.
Why can't they pick out men of leisure for such work,
And then if they don't come when called let them be fined.
It's surely work for men who eat their meals alone,
Who have no business, are not invited nor invite
To banquets—they should go to assemblies and elections.
If that were done I shouldn't have lost my feast today.
As sure as I am living he planned, I know, to give it.
At any rate I'll go: the thought of what's left delights me.
But look: I see Menaechmus with a wreathe on his head.
The banquet's over. By Pollux, I've caught him just in time.

Act III. Scene 2.

Men. 2.   Won't you be quiet if I'm to bring you back today
This cloak all splendidly fixed up in nick of time?
I'll fix it so you'll say it's not the same—disguised.
Pen.   He's taking the cloak to the dyer. The banquet's over,
The wine drunk up, the parasite shut out of doors.
By Hercules, I'm not the man I am unless
I get revenge for this. I'll watch what he will do
And afterwards I'll walk right up and speak to him.
Men. 2.   Ye gods above, to what man in a single day
Have you given more sheer good when he had hoped so little?
I've dined, I've drunk, I've bedded with a courtesan,
I've captured this that she shall never get again.
Pen.   I can't hear clearly from this distance what he says
But he is full of food and talks of me and mine.

Men. 2. She says I gave her this and that I stole it from
My wife. As soon as I had fallen to her error
Straightway, as though I'd had some business with her, I
Began to agree and whatsoever the woman said
I said the same. But what's the use of wasting words?
I never came off so well at quite so small expense.

Pen. It's time I approached him. I am keen to confound the man.

Men 2. Who's this now that approaches me?

Pen.   How say you, fellow?
Light as a feather, bad and a villain utterly,
You outrage of a man, tricky and worthless too?
What have I done that you should try to ruin me?
That you should slip away and lose me in the forum
And hold the funeral feast when I was far away?
Why did you dare to do it—I'm equally an heir.

Men. 2. Young man, I ask you, what have you to do with me?
That in your ignorance you curse an unknown man?
Or do you wish to suffer for your abusive words
Hereafter?

Pen.   Well, by Pollux, I know you gave her that.

Men. 2. Answer me now, young man, I ask you, what's your name?

Pen. Are you making fun of me as if you did not know?

Men. 2. By Pollux, as far as I know, up to this very day
I've never seen or known you but whoever you be
With any sense of justice you'd not be so hateful.

Pen. You don't know me?

Men. 2.   I wouldn't deny it if I did.

Pen. Menaechmus, come, wake up.

Men. 2.   I'm wide awake, I'm sane.

Pen. And still don't know your parasite?

Men. 2.   Young man, your brain
Is badly addled—of that fact I'm positive.

Pen. Answer me then this question. Did you not purloin
That cloak from your own wife to give to Erotium?

Men. 2. By Hercules, I have no wife and never gave
A thing to Erotium nor stole a cloak.

Pen.   Are you sane?

<pre>
             This matter is too much. Didn't I see you come
             Outdoors, dressed in the cloak?
Men. 2.   Curses upon your head!
             You think that every man's a pimp because you are.
             Do you assert that I was dressed up in this cloak?
Pen.   I do, by Hercules.
Men. 2.   Then go where you belong
             Or get yourself well purified, maddest of madmen.
Pen.   By Pollux, no man will ever persuade me not to tell
             Your wife the whole affair and how it was carried out
             And all your insults will come homing back to you.
             I'll do this: not without payment will you have eaten that feast.
Men. 2. What *is* all this that's happening? Every man I see
             Begins to mock me. But the door is creaking there.
</pre>

Act III. Scene 3.

<pre>
Maid   Menaechmus, your Erotium says she'd love to have
             You take this armlet right now to the jeweller
             And have him see to putting an ounce more gold in it
             And making the armlet just as good as when 'twas new.
Men. 2. Tell her that that and anything else she may desire
             I'll gladly carry out, whatever it be she wishes.
Maid   You know the armlet—what it is?
Men. 2.   No, save it's gold.
Maid   This is the armlet which you said you secretly
             Stole from the jewel casket of your loving wife.
Men. 2. Most certainly I did not.
Maid   You do not remember?
             Then give me back the armlet if you don't remember.
Men. 2. But stop, I do remember. This is one I gave her.
Maid   It is.
Men. 2.   Where are the others that I gave her with it?
Maid   You never gave her others.
Men. 2.   By Pollux, I guess you're right.
Maid   Shall I say you'll see to it?
</pre>

Men. 2.	Tell her it shall be duly done.
	The cloak and armlet both—I'll bring them back together.
Maid	I wish, Menaechmus mine, you'd have them make for me
	A pair of golden earrings—say, for about two crowns,
	So that I'd be real glad to see you when you come.
Men. 2.	It shall be done. Give me the money to pay for it.
Maid	You pay for it yourself—I'll pay you later on.
Men. 2.	No—come across.
Maid	I'll give you double by and by.
	I haven't got it.
Men. 2.	Well, when you have, then give it me.
Maid	Anything more?
Men. 2.	Yes, tell her I'll see to all of this

aside That they be sold for all that I can get for them.
Has she gone into the house? She's gone, the door is shut.
The gods are surely helping me with all their power.
But why am I lingering when the chance has come to me
With opportunity to escape this pander's haunt?
Hurry up, Menaechmus, shake a foot and show some speed.
I'll take this garland off and throw it here on the left
That anyone following may suppose I've gone that way.
And now I'll go and find, if possible, my servant
And let him know what blessings the gods have showered on me.

Act IV. Scene 1.

Wife of Men. 1.	Can I live on in wedlock such as we have here,
	When my husband steals in secret all that's in the house
	And carries it off to his mistress?
Pen.	Won't you shut your mouth.

I'll give you a chance to catch him openly. Just follow.
He was drunk with a garland on and taking to the dyer
That cloak he stole away from out your house today.
But look, there lies the garland. Am I a liar now?
And there he is, by Pollux, at just the proper time.
But he's not got the cloak.

Wife   What shall I say to him?
Pen.   Say what you always do—just bawl him out.
Wife   Good sense!
Pen.   But here! Let's hide away where we can watch from ambush.

Act IV.   Scene 2.

Men. 1. What a fool custom 'tis we always follow here
                And how nonsensical. Why, even the best of men,
                The very greatest, are guilty of this absurdity.
                For every one of us tries to have a lot of clients
                And whether they're good or bad we never make inquiry.
                It's wealth we look at rather than whether the client
                Has reputation of being a man of honesty.
                If he be poor but honest then he's thought quite worthless
                But if he's rich, why then we think him a perfect client.
                But those that never consider the law or ever think
                Of justice or of right—they keep their patrons nervous.
                They will deny they've given what they have; they're full
                Of law suits, men rapacious too and fraudulent
                Who out of money lending or by perjury
                Have made their fortune. So their claims are all they think of
                And when the day for trial is set, then straightaway
                The patrons they are summoned too and they must speak
                All in the client's cause who has offended, be it
                The case is heard before the people or a judge.
                And that is how a certain client has kept me busy
                Today and I have had no chance to do the things
                I wanted to, so busy he's kept me and distracted.
                The man was pleading before the aediles, having committed
                All kinds of vicious frauds. I interposed objections,
                Confused and tortuous. I orated not more nor less
                Of controversy than would gain a settlement.
                And he, what does he do but give it all away.
                I never saw a man so manifestly guilty.
                Three perfectly sound witnesses to every crime.

May all the gods destroy him for wasting so my day—
Destroy me too for ever setting eye on the forum.
I've spoiled the day, for I had ordered a splendid meal.
My mistress is expecting me, I know, and at
My first chance I have hurried here. I'm sure she's angry.
The cloak I gave her which I'd stolen from my wife
And gave Erotium, will appease her.

Pen.   What do you say to that?
Wife   I'm married to a villain.
Pen.   Could you hear him?
Wife   Enough.
Men. 1.   With any sense I'd enter where all's well.
Wife   Stop. Rather,
All's ill. By Castor, you took it at high cost.
Pen.   Take that.
Wife   Did you think you could do all that unknown to me?
Men. 1.   What troubles my wife?
Wife   You ask me?
Men. 1.   Shall I ask this fellow?
Pen.   Stop all that cooing. Go on, you.
Men. 1.   Why are you sore
At me?
Wife   You ought to know.
Pen.   He knows: he's just pretending.
Men. 1.   What's it about?
Wife   The cloak.
Men. 1.   The cloak?
Wife   The cloak.
Pen.   What scares you?
Men. 1.   I'm not at all scared but for this—the palla pales me.
Pen.   And didn't you eat the dinner without me? Keep at your man.
Men. 1.   Shut up!
Pen.   I won't shut up. He's nodding to stop my talking.
Men. 1.   By Hercules, I neither nodded nor winked at you.
Wife   By Castor, I'm a wretched woman.
Men. 1.   How wretched? Tell me.
Pen.   Nothing could be more blatant, denying what you saw.

Men. 1. By Jove and all the gods I swear, wife, (will that do?)
         I did not nod.
Pen.   All right, so be it. Come back to this.
Men. 1. To what?
Pen.   To the dyer's is my advice and bring the cloak back.
Men. 1. Cloak? What cloak?
Wife   I say no more. He's forgotten all.
Men. 1. Have some of the servants failed you? Or your maids? Or have
         The servants talked back? Tell me. They'll be punished.
Pen.   Nonsense.
Men. 1. You're downcast. That's not what I would have you be.
Pen.   Nonsense.
Men. 1. Or are you angry with someone of your friends?
Pen.   Nonsense.
Men. 1. You can't be out of sorts with me?
Pen.   No nonsense that.
Men. 1. By Pollux, I've done nothing to grieve you.
Pen.   Nonsense again.
Men. 1. Tell me, my wife, what's wrong with you?
Pen.   The beast's complacent.
Men. 1. Can't you stop being sore? I beg you.
Wife   Remove your hand.
Pen.   Take that! Now hurry and without me eat up the banquet,
         Garlanded, drunk, in front of the house make fun of me!
Men. 1. By Pollux, I have not dined nor entered here today.
Pen.   You deny it?
Men. 1.   Yes, by Hercules.
Pen.   None's bold as he.
         Didn't I see you here in front with a wreath of flowers?
         When you declared that I was not sound in the head?
         And said you did not know me—were a foreigner?
Men. 1. I should have left you long ago. I'm going home.
Pen.   I know. You thought I was not one to avenge myself.
         I've told all to your wife.
Men. 1.   Told what?
Pen.   I cannot say.
         Ask her yourself.

Men. 1.   What's this, my wife, this man has told you?
          What is it? Why silent? Speak up; tell me.
Wife   As if you knew not.
          You stole my cloak away from home.
Men. 1.   I stole your cloak?
Wife   You ask me that?
Men. 1.   I wouldn't if I knew.
Pen.   The villain!
          How he pretends. You just can't beat it. I knew all
          And told her everything.
Men. 1.   What is it?
Wife   Since you've no shame
          And won't of your own accord confess, listen to me:
          Why I am grim and what he said to me, I'll tell you.
          A cloak's been stolen from my home—
Men. 1.   A cloak from me?
Pen.   You see how captious he's become. From her, not you.
          For surely if 'twere stolen from you 'twould now be safe.
Men. 1.   I'm not addressing *you,* but what say *you*?
Wife   I say,
          It's stolen.
Men. 1.   Who stole it?
Wife   By Pollux, he knows that who stole it.
Men. 1.   But who?
Wife   A certain Menaechmus.
Men. 1.   Shameful business that.
          Who's this Menaechmus?
Wife   You, I say.
Men. 1.   Me?
Wife   You.
Men. 1.   Who says so?
Wife   I do.
Pen.   And I. And gave it to Erotium.
Men. 1.   I gave it?
Pen.   Yes, you, you, I say. You want an owl brought
          Who'll keep on saying, you, you to you? I'm getting tired.
Men. 1.   I swear by Jove and all the gods (is that enough?)

	My wife, I did not give it.
Pen.	*I* swear we're telling the truth.
Men. 1.	I didn't give it. I only loaned it to her to use.
Wife	By Castor, I don't give your coats and overcoats To anyone to use. It's for a woman to give away A woman's clothes, a man a man's. Will you bring it back?
Men. 1.	I'll do it. I'll bring it back.
Wife	For your own good, I'm sure, For you'll not enter this house unless the cloak comes too.
Men. 1.	I? House?
Pen.	And what do I get for the help I've given?
Wife	Your help will be returned when you have something stolen.
Pen.	And that, by Pollux, means never. I've nothing at home to lose. Well, damn you both then, man and wife. I'm for the forum, For I can see it. I've fallen out with this family.
Men. 1.	My wife thinks that she's done me ill in turning me out, As if I had no place to go, no better place. If I don't please *you,* well, I'll please Erotium. She'll not keep me away from her but shut me in. And now I'll ask her to give back the cloak I gave her. I'll buy her a better one. Hey there, someone. Janitor! Come, open up and call Erotium out to me.
Ero.	Who is it calls me?
Men. 1.	One more foe to himself than you.
Ero.	Menaechmus, why stand there outside: come follow me in.
Men. 1.	You know why I come here?
Ero.	Of course: to have joy of me.
Men. 1.	No, but that cloak I gave you some little time ago, Give it me back. My wife has found out everything. I'll buy you another, twice as costly, your own choice.
Ero.	But I gave it to you only now for the dying job, And the bracelet for the goldsmith to be changed in shape.
Men. 1.	*You* gave *me* the cloak and bracelet? No, you never did. Why, since I gave it you and departed for the forum, This is the first time I've returned.
Ero.	I see your game Because I gave them, you come back to cheat me here.

Men. 1. It's not to cheat that I ask them back, I swear.
       My wife's discovered all.
Ero.   I never in the first place
       Asked for it: of your own accord you gave it to me.
       And now you ask it back—all right, take it, wear it,
       Yourself or she, your wife, or lock it in a cupboard.
       Be sure of this: you'll never come to visit me
       Since you will treat so badly one who's been your friend.
       Bring me hard cash or never expect my favors more.
       Hereafter find another woman to cheat and fool.
Men. 1. You're far too testy. Here, I tell you, stop, come back.
       Wait! Aren't you willing even for my sake to return?
       She's gone inside and locked the door. I'm quite shut out.
       At home or with my mistress, no one believes my word.
       I'll go and find some friends to tell me what to do.

Act V. Scene 1.

Men. 2. I was an idiot when I gave my pocket book
       And money to my henchman, old Messenio.
       He's gone off somewhere, I suppose, to drown himself.
Wife   I'll watch and see how soon my husband will return.
       But look, I see him. I'm saved: he's got my cloak.
Men. 2. I wonder where Messenio has wandered off.
Wife   I'll go up to him with the greeting he deserves.
       Aren't you ashamed to appear here boldly in my sight?
       You outrage of a man, and with that cloak?
Men. 2.   What's got you?
       What's bothering you, my woman?
Wife   What now, impudent:
       You dare to utter a single syllable to me?
Men. 2. What have I done to you that I'd not dare to speak?
Wife   You dare to ask? The impudent boldness of the man!
Men. 2. Don't you know, woman, why the Greeks called Hecuba
       The dog?
Wife   I don't know and I do not want to know.

Men. 2. It was that Hecuba did what you are doing now:
          She always poured abuse on everyone she saw,
          And that's the reason why they rightly called her bitch.

Wife   I cannot any longer stand your loathesome conduct.
          I'd rather live without a husband all my life
          Than put up longer with the outrageous things you do.

Men. 2. What is it to me whether you stand your wedded life
          Or whether you leave your husband? Is it the custom here
          To tell your tattle to every stranger that you meet?

Wife   What tattle? I say I will no longer bear with it:
          I'll live divorced rather than stand your goings on.

Men. 2. As far as I'm concerned go on and be divorced,
          And stay so just as long as Jupiter is king.

Wife   But you denied to me you ever took my cloak
          And now you've got it here in sight. Aren't you ashamed;

Men. 2. By Hercules, my woman, you're bad and bold indeed.
          You dare to say I stole this cloak which only now
          Another woman gave me to have repaired for her?

Wife   By Castor, that's—but I'll go straight and call my father
          And tell him all the outrageous things you do to me.
          Here, Decio, go find my father out and bring him
          Back here with you to me. Tell him it's necessary.
          I'll tell him all your outrages.

Men. 2.   Is your mind sane?
          What is this outrageous business?

Wife   My cloak and jewels too
          You've stolen from your wife, from your own home,
          And given to your mistress. Is that idle prattle?

Men. 2. By Hercules, my woman, do you know some drug
          That I can take to help me bear your impudence?
          What man you take me for's a mystery to me:
          I knew you when I knew Porthaon of ancient times.

Wife   Laugh if you will at me—you cannot mock at him:
          My father's coming hither now. Come, look at him:
          Do you know *him*?

Men. 2.   Oh yes. I knew him when I knew Calchas.
          I saw *him* on the very day that I saw *you.*

Wife   You still deny that you know me nor yet my father?
Men. 2.   I'll say the same if you throw in your grandfather.
Wife   By Castor, that is just the way you're always acting.

Act. V.   Scene 2.

Father   Well, well, as far as age permits and times demand
         I'll step along. I'll go as fast as ever I can.
         But I know very well how fast that fast will be.
         I've lost my good old nimbleness: I'm all sewed up
         With age, I have a heavy body and all my strength
         Is gone. Ah me, old age is bad, a wretched bit of freight,
         For when it comes it brings along the worst of troubles.
         To tell them all at once would be a long, long story.
         But this is what at present is weighing on my mind:
         What in the world has happened now to make my daughter
         All of a sudden to send for me to come to her
         And does not tell me why she sends for me to come.
         But I've a pretty good notion what it's all about.
         I think it must be that she's quarreled with her husband.
         That's the way women do who want to make their men-folk
         Their slaves and, trusting in their dowry, get arrogant.
         And husbands too as well are often not blameless either
         And there's a limit to what a wife should put up with.
         And after all a daughter doesn't send for her father
         Unless there's something done or said to give good cause.
         Whatever it is I soon shall know for there she is
         Before the house—her husband also, looking sour.
         It's just as I suspected. Now I'll speak to her.
Wife   I'm going to meet him. Greetings to you, my father. Welcome.
Father   Greetings to you too. All is well that you have called me?
         Why then so gloomy? Why does he stand off in anger?
         You two have certainly been quarreling over something.
         Come, speak up. Who's to blame? Be brief: no long harangue.
Wife   I've never done a thing—on that I can relieve you.
         But I can't bear to live with that man any longer.

	Take me away.
Father	How's that?
Wife	I'm made a laughing stock.
Father	By whom?
Wife	By him, my husband whom you gave me to.
Father	Now look, a quarrel. How often have I said to you
	To watch your step, that neither come to me complaining.
Wife	But how, my father, can I help?
Father	You're asking me?
Wife	Yes, please.
Father	How many times have I explained to you
	Never to notice where he goes or what he does?
Wife	But he is making love to this whore, next door to us.
Father	Shrewd fellow! All the more he'll do it for your nagging.
Wife	He drinks there too.
Father	You think for you he'll drink the less
	If it please him either there or where he will? How silly!
	You might as well forbid his dining out or even
	Inviting company to dine with him at home.
	You want your husband then to be your humble slave?
	You might as well assign to him the daily housework
	And bid him sit among the maids to card the wool.
Wife	It looks as though I'd brought an advocate for him,
	Not for myself. I called—you plead for him.
Father	If he's
	At fault in anything, I'd be even more severe
	Than I have been with you. But while he keeps you well
	Supplied with clothes and jewelry and food and maids
	You'd better, woman, keep a saner attitude.
Wife	But he pilfers my chests of jewelry and cloaks
	Right from the house and secretly gives them to her.
Father	That's bad if he does that; if not it's you that's bad
	To accuse an innocent man.
Wife	But father, even now
	He has my cloak and bracelet which he gave to her
	And brings back now because he's been caught by me.
Father	I'll find out how that stands from him. I'll talk with him.

	Tell me, Menaechmus, why you two are quarreling.
	Why are you gloomy? Why does she stand off in anger?
Men. 2.	Whoever you are, old man, and what your name, I swear
	By Jove and all the gods—
Father	Swear what and what about?
Men. 2.	I never harmed this woman who now accuses me
	Of stealing from her house this cloak.
Wife	He swears to that?
Men. 2.	If ever I set foot within her house, I pray
	That I may be of all unhappy men most wretched.
Father	Are you now sane to pray that and to say that you
	Never set foot within the house where you are living?
Men. 2.	You say, old man, that I live here within that house?
Father	And you deny it?
Men. 2.	Yes, by Hercules.
Father	But falsely
	Unless you moved out overnight. Daughter, come here.
	What say you? Have you moved?
Wife	Moved where or why, I pray.
Father	I'm sure I don't know.
Wife	Father, he mocks you. Can't you see?
Father	Come, come, Menaechmus. Joking enough. Now come to business.
Men. 2.	Look here, what business have I got with you? Who are you?
	What do I owe you? Or yet her who keeps on nagging?
Wife	See you how green his eyes and how a greenish tinge
	Comes on his face and temples, how his eyes are flashing?
Men. 2.	What's better for me, since they seem to think I'm mad,
	Than to pretend I *am,* and so to keep them off?
Wife	See how he staggers and gapes. Father, what shall I do?
Father	Come here, my child, as far as possible from him.
Men. 2.	Euhoe Bacchus. Whither dost call me to hunt in the woods?
	I hear but at present I cannot abandon these regions about here
	While on my left that rabid bitch of a woman prevents
	And behind her stands a bald-headed goat who many a time
	Has ruined ere this by perjury many an innocent man.
Father	Curses upon your head!
Men. 2.	Behold from his oracle sacred

	Apollo bids me burn out her eyes with blazing brands.
Wife	Father, I'm lost. He threatens to burn out my two eyes.
Father	Daughter, look here.
Wife	What can we do?
Father	I'll call the servants.

I'll go and fetch some help to carry him home in chains
Before he makes more trouble here.

Men. 2.	Now then, I'm stuck.

Unless I first conceive a plan they'll carry me off.
You bid me not to spare my fists upon her face,
Apollo, unless she gets to the devil out of here?
I'll do your will.

Father	Get out as fast as ever you can

Before he beats you up.

Wife	I'm going but keep an eye

On him. Don't let him loose. Poor me, to hear such words.

Men. 2. Not badly, oh Apollo. Now for this most foul
        Tithonus, bearded, old and tremulous, who calls
        Himself the son of Cygnus. You command me crush
        His bones with that same staff he carries.

Father	You'll get hurt

If you lay hands on me or come the least bit nearer.

Men. 2. I'll do your bidding: with a double axe I'll hew
        This old man's flesh to pieces down to the very bone.

Father   I must look out. I must protect myself—I must.
        I'm really afraid he'll do me some harm the way he threatens.

Men. 2. You order many things, Apollo. You bid me yoke
        These steeds unbroken, fierce, to mount this chariot
        And dash to pieces this old stinking, toothless lion.
        Now am I in my car, now hold the reins, the goad
        Is in my hand. Up, steeds, now let your hooves ring out—
        Let not your speed relax but gallop straight at him.

Father   You threaten me with your yoked steeds?

Men. 2.	Behold, Apollo:

You bid me charge at him who stands there now and kill him.
But who now drags me by the hair from out the car
And so revokes your orders and Apollo's will?

Father   By Hercules, how fierce an attack was that! Ye gods!
         This crazy man was perfectly well a while ago
         And suddenly this violent seizure falls on him.
         I'll go and fetch a doctor just as fast as I can.

Act V.   Scene 3.

Men. 2. They've really gone and vanished wholly from my sight
         That forced me, sane as any man else, to play the madman?
         I'd better be off to join my ship while still I can.
         I beg you all, if that old man should come back here,
         Don't tell him in what direction I have gone away. *Exit.*
Father   My buttocks ache from sitting and my eyes from watching
         While waiting for the doctor to come back from calls.
         But finally the old bore did come back from his patients.
         He says he set a leg for Aesclapius
         And then an arm for Apollo till I'm wondering
         Whether to say I've got a doctor or mechanic.
         Look at him plodding along. Come, hustle a bit that ant's pace.

Act V.   Scene 4.

Doctor   Well now, old man, what said you was the character
         Of his attack? Possessed of demons or just off his head?
         Lethargic or some fluid subcutaneous?
Father   That's what I brought you here for: to tell me those things
         And make him well again.
Doctor   Oh, that's nothing at all.
         I give you my word of honor: he'll be well again.
Father   I want him to be treated with the greatest care.
Doctor   Why, I will sigh more than six hundred times a day.
         That's how much care I'll give to make him well again.
Father   Ah, there's the man himself. Let's watch what he will do.

Act V. Scene 5.

Men. 1. By Pollux, this has been a day when all's gone wrong.
         All that I thought was well concealed that parasite
         Has now revealed. He's my Ulysses who concocts
         All evil for his king. Sure as I live I'll end
         That fellow's life. But I'm a fool to call it his
         When it's my own. My food and money reared him. Now
         I'll kill the man. As for this harlot, she but plays
         Her part. Because I ask her to let me take the cloak
         Back to my wife, she says she gave it to me. Ye gods!
         By Pollus, I surely am a really wretched man.

Father   Can you hear what he says?

Doctor   He says he's wretched.

Father   Go up to him.

Doctor   Good day, Menaechmus, why do you bare your arms like that?
         Don't you then know how bad that is for your disease?

Men. 1. Go hang yourself.

Father   Do you notice anything?

Doctor   I should say
         I do. This case can not be handled with a load
         Of hellebore. But say, man.

Men. 1.   What do you want?

Doctor   Just tell me this:
         Do you drink white wine or the red?

Men. 1.   You go to hell.

Doctor   He's showing now the first signs of insanity.

Men. 1. Why don't you ask if I eat purple bread or red?
         Or yellow? Birds with scales or fish with wings?

Father   Dear me!
         You hear his wildly raving talk. Why don't you give
         Some potion? If you don't he'll go entirely mad.

Doctor   Just wait. I've more to ask.

Men. 1.   You're killing me with your babble.

Doctor   Now tell me, do your eyes ever turn quite hard?

Men. 1. Do you take me for a lobster, good-for-nothing?

Doctor   And do your bowels ever rumble noticeably?

Men. 1. Not when I've had my fill, but, when I'm hungry, yes.
Doctor In that reply there's surely no insanity.
        Do you sleep through the night and go to sleep with ease?
Men. 1. I sleep right through if I've paid all the debts I owe.
        May Jupiter and all the gods damn you, inquisitor!
Doctor Now he sounds really mad. After those words look out.
Father Oh no. Compared with what he was he sounds like Nestor.
        A while ago he called his wife a rabid bitch.
Men. 1. What! I?
Father   You said it while you raved.
Men. 1.   I did?
Father   Yes, you.
        And threatened to run me down with a four-horse chariot.
        I saw all this and I'm the man that's accusing you.
Men. 1. And I know that you purloined the crown of Jupiter.
        I know that you were put in prison for that crime,
        And when you came out I know you were whipped in stocks,
        And then I know you killed your father and sold your mother.
        Do I repay you for your abuse like a sane man?
Father I beg you, doctor, whatever you're going to do, do quickly.
        Can you not see he's crazy?
Doctor   I know what you'd better do.
        Have him brought to my house.
Father   That's your advice?
Doctor   Why not?
        There I can treat the man as I find best.
Father   So be it.
Doctor You shall drink hellebore, on order, for twenty days.
Men. 1. I'll string you up and stick you with goads for thirty days.
Doctor Go call some men to carry him to my house.
Father   How many?
Doctor Considering how mad he is, say four at least.
Father They'll be here soon. Watch him well, doctor.
Doctor   Nay, I'll go home
        To get all ready that's essential. Order your slaves
        To bring him to me.
Father   I'll do that.

Doctor   I'm off.
Father   Farewell.
Men. 1. Father-in-law's gone, doctor's gone. Alone, by god.
         Why is it that these men all declare that I am mad?
         For since the day that I was born I've never been sick
         Nor am I mad nor look for fights nor stir·up quarrels.
         I'm sound, find others sound, I recognise my friends,
         I chat with them. Are these men mad that call me mad?
         What shall I do? I'd like to go home. My wife won't have it.
         And as for here, no one will let me in. It's horrible.
         Here I'll remain forever. Perhaps at night they'll let me in.

Act V.   Scene 6.

Mes.   This is your test of a good servant, if he always watches
         His master's interests, gives them his diligent care
         And keen consideration, in his master's absence
         Watches his master's business just as carefully
         As when he's present or more so. If his heart is right
         He'll surely think more of his back than of his gullet,
         More of his shanks than of his belly. He'd best remember
         How good for nothing, lazy fellows are rewarded
         By masters: whippings and chains, work at the mill, all these
         Are the reward of laziness. I'm mortally afraid
         Of such reward and that is why I mean to live
         A good life rather than a bad. Scolding I'll take;
         Whipping I can't abide and I prefer to eat
         The meal rather than turn the mill. So I obey
         My master's orders strictly and I find it pays.
         Others may do as they will, I'll treat my master rightly.
         I'll have a proper fear, keep clear of blame, behaving
         Always as I should for master's sake. Then soon
         I shall have my reward. My principle's to work
         As is the best for my own back. I've left the luggage
         And with it the slaves as master bade me at the inn
         And now I come to join him. I'll knock on the door

To let him know I'm here and then I'll take him safely
Out of this den of thieves. But I'm afraid that I
Have come too late to find the battle over and done.

Act V.   Scene 7.

Father By gods and men I charge you that you follow well
The orders that I've given you and now repeat.
Pick up that man at once and carry him to the doctor's
Unless you have no care for your own flanks and legs.
And see you give no heed to any threats he makes.
Why stand you still? Why hesitate? Come, hoist him up.
I'll to the doctor's to be there when you arrive.

Men. 1. Murder! What is this? Why are those fellows rushing at me?
What do you want? What are you after? Why surround me?
Where are you pulling me? Where taking me? Help! Help!
I call on you, ye citizens of Epidamnus.

Mes. Ye gods above! What's going on before my eyes?
My master carried off by unknown ruffians!

Men. 1. Will no one help me?

Mes. I will, master and most boldly.
Oh, what an outrage! Citizens of Epidamnus,
What outrage! Here's my master in a peaceful city,
A peaceful visitor, in daylight on the street
Abducted. Here, let go of him.

Men. 1. Whoever you are
I beg you to help me. Don't let me be so maltreated.

Mes. Not I! I'll help defend you with the best of heart.
I'll never let you perish—better to die myself.
Master, gouge out that fellow's eye that's holding you.
For these, I'll sow a harvest of fists upon their faces.
By Hercules, you'll pay for this. Let go of him.

Men. 1. I've got his eye.

Mes. Then make the socket hole show well.
You villains, bandits, robbers. All is up with us.

Slave I beg—

Mes.   Let go.
Men. 1.   What do you mean by touching me?
               Comb him well with your fists.
Mes.   Get out and go to the devil.
               There's one for you, a prize for being last to go.
               I marked their faces very well, quite to my taste.
               By Pollux, master, I arrived in nick of time.
Men. 1. God bless you richly, whosoever you may be,
               For without you I'd never have lived to see the sun set.
Mes.   By Pollux, then, master, you should surely set me free.
Men. 1. *I* set *you* free?
Mes.   But, master, I saved your life.
Men. 1.   What's this?
               Young man, you're wrong.
Mes.   I wrong?
Men. 1.   By father Jupiter,
               I swear I'm not your master.
Mes.   Oh, come now.
Men. 1.   'Tis true.
               No slave of mine has ever done so much for me.
Mes.   Then if you say I'm not your slave, why, set me free.
Men. 1. As far as I'm concerned, go free whenever you will.
Mes.   That's orders?
Men. 1.   Yes, by Hercules, if I've the right.
Mes.   Hail then, my patron, hail. "Since you are free, Messenio,
               I do rejoice." And I believe you but I beg of you,
               Give me your orders as when I was still your slave.
               I'll live with you and when you leave go home with you.
Men. 1. *aside* Oh no, you won't.
Mes.   I'll go to the tavern and collect
               The baggage and the cash. The wallet, safely sealed,
               With the money in the bag, I'll bring it you.
Men. 1.   Yes, do.
Mes.   I'll bring it intact just as you gave it. Wait for me here.
Men. 1. How strangely things are falling out for me today.
               Some say I'm not myself and shut me out of doors
               While this man says he'll bring me money and was my slave,

My servitor to whom I gave his liberty.
He says besides he'll bring a wallet with money in it.
If he does that I'll bid him go wherever he will
Away from me, lest, when he's sane, he ask it back.
Father-in-law and doctor said I'm mad. I don't know
What it all means. It's just as bad as dreaming dreams.
Now I'll go in and join this harlot, though she's angry,
And try to get back the cloak and take it home with me.

Act V. Scene 8.

Men. 2. You brazen fool. You dare to say we've met today
Since I commanded you to meet me here?
Mes.   But yes—
I broke in when four men were carrying you away
Before this house and you were calling on gods and men
When I came up and saved you in a good hard fight.
And that was why—because I saved you—you set me free.
Then when I said I'd fetch the money and the bags
You ran to meet me and deny what you had done.
Men. 2. So I set you free?
Mes.   You certainly did.
Men. 2.   The surest thing
Is that I'd be a slave before I'd set you free.

Act V. Scene 9.

Men. 1. Swear on by what you will: you cannot prove thereby
I ever took away that cloak and bracelet, you graceless slut.
Mes.   Ye gods above, what am I seeing?
Men. 2.   What do you see?
Mes.   Your mirror.
Men. 2.   What do you mean?
Mes.   Your image. Couldn't be clearer.
Men. 2. By Pollux, he's not unlike me when I consider myself.

Men. 1. Hey there, young man that saved my life, whoever you are.
Mes.   Young sir, I beg you, tell me your name if you don't mind.
Men. 1. By Pollux, you don't deserve of me that I should grudge
        To tell you that. My name's Menaechmus.
Men. 2.   No, that's mine.
Men. 1. I come from Syracuse, in Sicily.
Men. 2.   That's my home too.
Men. 1. What's that?
Men. 2.   A fact.
Mes.   I know this man. He is my master.
        And I'm *his* slave but fancied I belonged to *him.*
        I thought that he was you, sir, and I made him trouble.
        I beg your pardon, sir, if I've said anything silly.
Men. 2. You're talking like a perfect fool. Don't you remember
        You landed from the ship with me today?
Mes.   That's right.
        Then *you* are my master. Hail to *you*—farewell to *you*.
        This man's Menaechmus.
Men. 1.   No, *I* am.
Men. 2.   What nonsense's this?
        You are Menaechmus?
Men. 1.   So I say, the son of Moschus.
Men. 2. My father's son?
Men. 1.   Not so, young man; *my* father's son.
        I've no desire to take away *your* father from you.
Mes.   Ye gods above, grant me the hope I think I see.
        For unless my mind deceives me these are the two twin brothers.
        For what they say of country tallies and of father.
        I'll call my master aside. Menaechmus—
Men. 1.
and 2.   Yes?
Mes.   Not both.
        The one of you that came with me on the ship.
Men. 1.   Not me.
Men. 2. 'Twas me.
Mes.   I want you then. Come here.
Men. 2.   I've come. What is it?

Mes.   That man over there is either a swindler or your twin brother.
I never saw a man so like another man.
Two drops of milk or water aren't any more alike
Than he's like you and you like him. And then he says
His country's name, his father's are the same as yours.
We'd better go to him right away and question him.

Men. 2. By Hercules, you're right in that advice. I'm grateful.
Keep up your help, I pray. You're free if you find out
That he's my brother.

Mes.   So I hope to do.

Men. 2.   Me too.

Mes.   What say you there? I think you said your name's Menaechmus?

Mcn. 1. I did.

Mes.   And he's Menaechmus too. In Sicily,
At Syracuse you said you were born. The same with him.
You said your father's name was Moschus. So was his.
You both can do me a good turn—yourselves as well.

Men. 1. You've earned the right to ask me what you will and get it.
And though I'm free I'll serve you like a paid-for slave.

Mes.   My hope is I shall find you two are brother twins,
Born of one mother and one father on one day.

Men. 1. A strange tale that. I wish you could fulfill your promise.

Mes.   I can. But come now, both of you, answer my questions.

Men. 1. Ask what you will. I'll answer everything I know.

Mes.   Your name's Menaechmus?

Men. 1.   It is.

Mes.   And yours, is it the same?

Men. 2. It is.

Mes.   Your father's name was Moschus?

Men. 1.   Yes.

Men. 2.   And mine.

Mes.   You were from Syracuse?

Men. 1.   Of course.

Mes.   And you?

Men. 2.   Of course.

Mes.   The evidence so far is sure. Attention now.
What is the farthest back, at home, you can remember?

Men. 1. I left Tarentum on a business trip with father
       And got lost in the crowd and then was lugged away.
Men. 2. Great Jupiter preserve me.
Mes.   Why the noise? Keep quiet.
       How old were you then when your father sailed away?
Men. 1. Seven I was, for then my teeth were falling out.
       And after that I never saw my father.
Mes.   Tell me
       How many sons he had.
Men. 1.   As I remember, two.
Mes.   And which of you was elder?
Men. 1.   We were just the same.
Mes.   How could that be?
Men. 1.   We both were twins.
Men. 2.   The gods have saved me.
Mes.   If you break in I'll stop.
Men. 1.   I'm silent.
Mes.   Tell me now
       Had you the same name, both?
Men. 1.   Oh no. Mine was the same
       As now, Menaechmus. He was then called Sosicles.
Men. 2. I see it all. I can't hold back. I must embrace him—
       My own twin brother, hail to you. I'm Sosicles.
Men. 1. How got you later then this other name, Menaechmus?
Men. 2. When we were sent the word that you and father were dead,
       Grandfather changed my name, gave me what had been yours.
Men. 1. I must believe what you have said but tell me—
Men. 2.   Yes?
Men. 1. What was our mother's name?
Men. 2.   Taximarche.
Men. 1.   That's right.
       Oh hail! To see you after all these years unhoped for.
Men. 2. And you too, brother. I'm so glad to find you now
       After these many wretched toils in looking for you.
Mes.   That's why this wench here called you by your brother's name.
       She took you for him when she asked you in for dinner.
Men. 1. By Pollux, I did tell them to prepare a dinner

	In secret from my wife whose cloak I stole from home
	And gave to her.
Men. 2.	This cloak that I have here?
Men. 1.	That's it.
	But how came you to get it?
Men. 2.	The wench invited me
	To dinner. She said I gave it to her. I dined right well,
	Drank well, enjoyed the wench, received the cloak and bracelet.
Men. 1.	By, Pollux, I'm glad you got some fun on my account,
	For when she bade you in she must have thought 'twas me.
Mes.	You've no objection to my going free as promised?
Men. 1.	A just and fair request, my brother. Do it for me.
Men. 2.	Go free.
Men. 1.	I'm very glad you're free, Messenio.
Mes.	But I need better auspices to be free for good.
Men. 2.	Brother, since all's come out to our dearest expectation,
	Let us return to our country.
Men. 1.	I'll do as you say.
	I'll hold an auction here, sell all I have. But now
	Come in with me.
Men. 2.	Of course.
Mes.	You know what I would like?
Men. 1.	What then?
Mes.	Make me the auctioneer.
Men. 1.	All right.
Mes.	Shall I
	Announce at once the auction?
Men. 1.	Yes, for a week from now.
Mes.	There'll be an auction here a week hence in the morning.
	For sale: the slaves, house, land and furniture. For sale
	At your own price—but money down. If anyone wishes
	He'll sell his wife. I don't believe the whole affair
	Will come to more than perhaps five hundred sesterces.

And now, spectators, fare ye well. Give your applause.

The end.

Index of Authors And Their Works